I0079666

One Blind Spot—
How Convexity Changes Everything

FⅢR
The
Freeman
Institute
for Integrative
Research

Eric J. Freeman, PhD

FⅢR
The
Freeman
Institute
for Integrative
Research

Copyright © 2025 by Eric J. Freeman
All rights reserved.

Published by
FIIR Press
The Freeman Institute for Integrative Research
201 Columbia Mall Blvd.
Columbia, SC 29223

ISBN 979-8-9929512-5-7

No part of this publication may be reproduced, distributed, or
transmitted in any form or by any means, including photocopying,
recording, or other electronic or mechanical methods, without the prior
written permission of the publisher, except in the case of brief quotations
embodied in critical reviews and certain other noncommercial uses
permitted by copyright law.

First Edition

Table of Contents

FⅢR
The
Freeman
Institute
for Integrative
Research

This book is a product of The Freeman Institute for Integrative Research—an interdisciplinary initiative committed to bridging rigorous theological study with real-world application. The Institute exists to make doctrine accessible, elevate historically marginalized voices, and provide believers with spiritually formative resources that speak to the challenges of contemporary life.

One Blind Spot: How Convexity Changes Everything embodies the Institute's mission by providing a theologically grounded and psychologically informed framework for seeing ourselves and our world more clearly. This book offers an emotionally honest tool designed to nurture the self-awareness and spiritual maturity necessary for a life of integrity and purpose.

To learn more or access additional resources, visit:

EricJFreeman.com

Dedicated to my father,

The Rev. Moses Elijah Freeman, Jr.

September 5, 1935 – April 4, 2015

Preface
Just One Blind Spot

A life rarely changes all at once. More often, it pivots on a single, humbling moment of clarity. It is the sudden, sharp realization that the way we have been seeing the world is not the way the world actually is. This book is about that moment. It is built on a single conviction: that learning to see and adjust for just one blind spot can set in motion a profound transformation and open us up to a deeper, more honest way of moving through our lives.

My own journey into this truth did not begin in a place of spiritual triumph, but in a moment of near disaster on a Florida highway. It was the fall of 2014, and I was serving as my ailing father's caretaker. From the passenger seat of my blue sports coupe, a relic from my former corporate life, he witnessed what I could not: a car hidden in the massive blind spot of my vehicle, one I was seconds away from hitting. My mirror told me the lane was clear; reality was about to prove my mirror wrong.

Later that day, he did not focus on my failure; instead, he addressed my defensiveness. With the quiet grace that defined his life, he stood by the car and offered a diagnosis that would change mine. "The problem isn't that you're not looking," he told me. "The problem is that this mirror isn't letting you *see*." He then handed me a simple tool: a small, convex mirror. That tiny, curved piece of glass did not change the world around me, but it fundamentally changed my ability to see it. It gave me a wider field of vision. It gave me the margin to move with awareness, rather than just confidence.

That experience became the central metaphor for this book. I began to see that we all navigate life with "flat mirrors," ingrained perspectives that are too narrow to reveal the whole truth. The principle I have come to call *Convexity* is the discipline of adding that curve: a grace-shaped way of seeing that is wider, humbler, and truer to reality.

This book is a practical tool designed to help you find and install your own convex mirror. We will explore the blind spots that show up in every area of our lives: the emotional, the rational, the relational, and the spiritual. Drawing on insights from theology, psychology, and personal experience, we will learn to identify the unwritten scripts and unquestioned assumptions that shape our lives, often without our awareness.

This is not a journey to be rushed. In the appendix, you will find "The Convexity Journal," a guided companion designed to help you pause and apply these ideas to your own life. My hope is that by engaging with these pages honestly, you will be able to name a blind spot you were previously unaware of and, in doing so, discover a new and liberating clarity.

We do not need a whole new life; we just need a better view. Let us begin the work of adjusting the mirror.

—*Dr. Eric J. Freeman*

Part I – Understanding the Spot

Chapter 1

The Spot

What You Can't See Can Still Steer Your Life

I used to believe I had a pretty good sense of my surroundings. Especially behind the wheel. I had a confidence born from years of driving, a kind of practiced certainty you don't question until you are forced to. My vehicle at the time was a blue 2005 Lexus SC430, a sleek sports coupe that was a carryover from my former life in corporate America and the pharmaceutical industry. For nearly five years, it had been my trusted companion on the road, and I thought I knew its every response, its every angle. I knew the road. I trusted my instincts. I followed the rules. I even signaled early. What I did not know, however, is that you can check your mirrors, do everything right, and still miss what is right next to you.

The lesson that would change everything arrived with a jolt on a Florida highway in the fall of 2014. I was in my early forties and was serving as my father's primary caretaker during a difficult season for his health. We were driving down Highway 60 in Brandon, and I was in the passing lane, looking to move right. I checked my mirror, saw what I perceived to be a clear lane, and began to merge. Suddenly, my father's sharp, urgent warning cut through the quiet hum of the car. I had not seen it, but he had. A young driver in an older, grey Honda Accord was right there, occupying the very space I was about to enter. My father had noticed the vehicle before its driver even had time to react to my mistake.

I swerved back into my lane, my heart pounding in my chest. A wave of hot frustration washed over me, immediately followed by the chilling realization of what could have happened. It was a close call, the kind that leaves you shaken and replaying the moment in your mind. I was frustrated, blaming the other driver in my head, blaming the road, blaming anything but the real source of the problem. I did not see it. Literally.

That is the profound danger of a blind spot: it does not feel like neglect on our part. It feels like certainty. It does not ask you to doubt what you see; it quietly and completely hides what you do not.

Later that evening, back at the house, the weight of the near-accident still lingered in the air between us. My father, whose body was ailing but whose spirit was as sharp and present as ever, walked me back out to the car. He offered no lecture, no interrogation, only his quiet presence. He walked to the passenger side and tapped lightly on the mirror.

"That coupe has a huge B-pillar blind spot," he said, his voice strong not with volume, but with a familiar tone of certainty and care that I had known my whole life.

I was defensive before I was curious. It's a natural human reaction when our competence is challenged. "I check the mirror every time," I insisted.

"I know you do," he replied gently, and in those four words, he disarmed all my defensiveness. "The problem isn't that you're not looking. The problem is that this mirror isn't letting you *see*. A flat mirror can only show you so much."

He then went inside the house and returned a moment later from his study, holding a small, round object in his hand.

It was a new convex mirror, still in its plastic seal. Apparently, he kept extras around, a testament to his own practical wisdom.

"We're going to put this right here," he said, carefully peeling the adhesive backing and placing it on the lower corner of my side mirror. He adjusted it ever so slightly. "There. Now watch what happens next time." It did not look like much, just a tiny curve of glass. But something in his voice, a quiet authority, told me this was not optional.

The next morning, I got in the car and backed out like usual. The roads were the same. The traffic was no different. But now, because of that small, curved piece of glass, there was more to see. I saw the car in the next lane long before it was in my way. I saw the cyclist I might have otherwise crowded. I saw the pedestrian stepping off the curb with time to spare. None of them had been invisible the day before; I just had not had the right angle to notice them. The strangest thing happened: my frustration lifted. I was not on edge. I was not angry. I was not guessing anymore. I was simply aware.

The Certainty of What We Do Not See

That little mirror, so small it seemed insignificant, revealed what had always been there. It did not change the road. It did not change the traffic. It did not change the people around me. It changed me. It taught me a simple but profound lesson that day: what you do not see can still steer your life. A blind spot does not have to be malicious to be dangerous. It does not have to be intentional to cause harm. It just has to be unnoticed. For a long time, I had thought the lane was clear because the mirror said so. I trusted the angle. I trusted the frame. But the frame was too narrow, and the mirror too flat. My certainty was just another form of blindness.

In that moment, the car became a classroom. And that mirror became a metaphor. I began to wonder: What else in my life had I misread because my view was too narrow? What else had I blamed on others because I could not see clearly? And perhaps most importantly: How often had I mistaken frustration for discernment, when all I needed was a better mirror? The longer I sat with that mirror in my side view, the more it started speaking to me without saying a word. It told the truth without apology. It did not flatter. It did not argue. It simply revealed. And the more it revealed, the more I had to reckon with what I had missed and why I had missed it.

It was not that I was reckless. I was confident. And that was part of the problem. The blind spot was so dangerous precisely because it hid behind my sense of competence. I believed I had everything under control, and that belief insulated me from curiosity. If I had been uncertain, I might have double-checked. But certainty is a powerful thing. It makes us stop asking questions. That mirror made me ask again.

Most people never discover their blind spots on their own. It usually takes a confrontation: an accident, a consequence, a loss, a moment of feedback you did not ask for but cannot forget. Something unexpected enters your field of experience and refuses to be ignored. And if you are humble enough, you will pause long enough to consider: Maybe the problem was not them. Maybe I did not see it clearly.

What surprised me most was how unremarkable the fix had been. There was no overhaul, no trip to the body shop. It was just a simple, curved mirror, barely the size of a silver dollar. But its shape changed everything. It made me see more, not because it was larger, but because it was convex. That curve, that outward bend, that subtle expansion of the reflective surface suddenly widened my field of view. What had been hidden was now visible. That small adjustment made a massive difference. It gave me the luxury of time, the chance to respond, and the ability to stay in my lane and honor the presence of what was beside me.

What changed was not my eyes. It was my angle.

There is a concept in psychology known as inattentional blindness. In short, it is the failure to notice something that is right in front of you when your attention is focused elsewhere. The most famous experiment involves participants watching a video of people passing basketballs. Halfway through, a person in a gorilla suit walks right through the scene, pounds their chest, and walks off. When asked about it later, nearly half of the viewers say they never saw the gorilla at all.[1] Why? Because they were so focused on counting passes that they filtered out everything else.

Our brains are masters of filtering. They have to be. We are bombarded with information, with sounds, colors, movements, micro-expressions, smells, and signals, and we simply cannot process it all at once. So the brain relies on filters. It highlights what seems relevant and discards the rest. It assumes you will only want to notice what you have told it is important. At the core of this process is something called the Reticular Activating System or RAS.[2] It is a bundle of nerves at the base of your brainstem that decides what stimuli get through to your conscious awareness and what gets screened out. It is the reason you can tune out background noise but instantly hear your name across a crowded room. It is why, after you buy a new car, you start seeing that model everywhere. You did not suddenly become more observant. Your brain just learned to prioritize that detail.

The RAS is brilliant. But it is also biased. It shows you what your subconscious has learned to value. It will always filter the world to match your expectations. If you assume people are untrustworthy, you will only notice the times they fail. If you believe you are always being overlooked, your brain will highlight every moment you do not get picked. If you think nothing ever goes your way, your perception will adjust to support that narrative until it feels like reality.

A Mirror for the Soul

But perception is not just perception. It is direction. Because what you see determines where you go and what you avoid. That is why Convexity matters. Convexity is not just a physical curve; it is a mental and spiritual one. It is a way of bending your perception so that it includes more than just what you were conditioned to notice. It is not that the mirror sees more; it just shows more. It reminds you that your default view is incomplete, no matter how confident you feel. Convexity says: *Slow down. You might not be seeing everything.* In a world that rewards speed and certainty, that kind of posture is not just rare; it is revolutionary.

What started as a driving correction became a personal conviction. I realized how much of my life I had been navigating through flat mirrors, mirrors that reflected just enough to keep me functional, but not enough to make me faithful. They worked fine, until they did not. They gave me confidence, until confidence turned to collision. And what convicted me most was not just how much I had missed; it was how long I had misdiagnosed the problem. I though the road was dangerous. I thought the other drivers were reckless. I thought the tension was always somewhere out there. But it was not. The blind spot was in me.

Once I saw it, I could not unsee it. Not just in my car, but in my conversations, in my assumptions, in my disappointments, in my leadership, and in my faith. I started to notice moments where I was reacting to what I did not fully understand, moments when I had made judgments based on partial information, moments when I had written someone off without asking why they moved the way they did. The mirror taught me to pause before I merged. And that pause, brief though it was, began to teach my soul how to check again, to look again, and to wait just long enough for a fuller view.

In Scripture, there is a haunting line repeated by the prophets and echoed by Jesus: "They have eyes, but do not see." That is not about physical vision. That is about spiritual posture. It is a warning that you can be devout and still blind. That you can be committed to God and still miss the movement of God. That you can know doctrine and still distort truth because your frame is too narrow. Moral vision is never just about information. It is about formation. It is about how you were shaped to see, and whether you are willing to unlearn what needs to be unlearned.

Think about the older brother in the parable of the prodigal son. He had done everything right. He stayed home, worked hard, and obeyed the rules. But the moment grace entered the picture, grace for someone he did not think deserved it, his vision narrowed. He refused to go inside, refused to celebrate, refused to see his brother as family. Why? Because his mirror was too flat. He thought obedience guaranteed blessing, that discipline entitled him to favor. He had no room in his theology for restoration that was unearned. And so he stayed outside, close to the house and close to the father, but far from the heart of grace.

Convexity would have bent his view. It would have helped him see his brother differently, see himself differently, and see the father's mercy more clearly. But flat mirrors do not make room for the unexpected. They only reflect what confirms what we already believe. That is the tragedy of unexamined blind spots: they make grace feel offensive, and others feel disposable.

But here is the mercy of it all: God gives us mirrors. Sometimes they come in the form of people. Sometimes in moments of failure. Sometimes in sudden flashes of insight or the gentle voice of a friend who loves you enough to tell you the truth. And sometimes, if you are fortunate, they come in the form of a father in your driveway, handing you a small, convex mirror, not to scold you, but to save you. Because what you do not see can still hurt you. And what you do not see can still hurt someone else.

Convexity is not a magic solution. It does not remove the blind spot completely. But it changes how you relate to it. It changes your posture. It invites you to move with humility, to live with room for more than your default frame. It teaches you that clarity is not just about information; it is about the willingness to adjust. So here is where we begin, not with shame, but with awareness. You do not have to see everything. But you do have to acknowledge there is more to see. You do not need a whole new life. But you may need a better mirror. A curved one. A deeper one. One shaped not by your assumptions, but by grace.

Let us adjust it, together.

Now that we have seen how a single blind spot can steer our lives, it is time to look closer at the solution. The power was not just in having another mirror; it was in its unique shape, a curve that introduces the powerful principle I have come to call Convexity.

Endnotes

1. Simons, Daniel J., and Christopher F. Chabris. "Gorillas in Our Midst: Sustained Inattentional Blindness for Dynamic Events." *Perception*, vol. 28, no. 9, 1999, pp. 1059–1074.

2. Baars, Bernard J., and Nicole M. Gage. *Fundamentals of Cognitive Neuroscience: A Beginner's Guide*. Academic Press, 2010.

Chapter 2

Convexity

The Shape of a Better Way of Seeing

When I first installed that small convex mirror on my Lexus, I did not realize it would change more than my driving. It was not a high-tech or expensive device. It required no complex instruction manual. It was just curved. And that simple curve turned out to be the difference between almost crashing on a Florida highway and calmly navigating forward. At first, I thought the mirror simply added more data to my field of vision. But over time, as the metaphor of that mirror began to seep into other areas of my life, I realized it was doing something far more profound. It was not just showing me more; it was training me to look differently. The mirror did not change the road. It changed my readiness for it. It expanded what I could notice without rushing, without panicking, and without missing something vital that was just outside my normal frame of reference.

That is when I first understood: the power of that mirror was not just in its clarity. It was in its convexity.

The mirror curved outward, and that single, subtle curve altered everything. It allowed for a wider field of vision without making the objects within it appear distorted. It bent the boundaries of my sight just enough to account for what was near, even if it was not yet visible in a flat, direct reflection. It did not exaggerate reality; it simply adjusted my ability to perceive it. It gave me more grace to respond and more time to merge. Ultimately, it gave me more margin to move. Convexity became the metaphor I did not know I needed, not just for driving, but for discernment, for leadership, for love. It taught me that we do not always need sharper eyes. Sometimes, we just need a better shape of mirror.

This is what this chapter is about. It is not about a product, but a posture. Not a gadget, but a grace. It is about a way of seeing that reflects humility instead of hurry, wholeness instead of ego, and reality instead of assumption. It is about learning to live with a convex way of seeing.

A Wider Frame for the World

The car mirror was just the beginning. I experienced this same shift years later while traveling. I was standing in a customs line in East Africa, and the officer asked me a routine question: "What nation are you from?"

"America," I answered automatically, with the certainty of someone who has answered that question the same way his entire life.

The officer paused, looked at me, and replied, "Which America? And which nation?"

It took me a moment to process his words. In that instant, my perspective, which had been so flat and singular, was forced to curve. Of course, he was right. There is North America and South America. And within those continents are dozens of distinct nations. My default answer assumed that my identity as an "American" was a universally understood monolith. His question introduced a wider, more complex, and more accurate field of view. He handed me a verbal convex mirror. Nothing about me had changed, but in that moment, how I saw my place in the world was forever adjusted.

This is what Convexity does. It is what happens when you allow God, sometimes through the gentle probe of a stranger, to reshape your perception so that it reflects not just what you have learned, but what you have been missing. Most of us are shaped by flat mirrors, by frameworks that only reflect what affirms our limited view. We listen to news that confirms our conclusions. We build friendships with people who echo our assumptions. We defend our way of seeing without asking whether we were taught to see poorly in the first place. Flat mirrors build confidence. Convex mirrors build capacity.

Convexity is not natural; it is learned. And it often begins with discomfort. Think of a long-standing family tradition, one that has been observed the same way for generations. When a younger member suggests a change, the first reaction from the others is often not curiosity, but resistance. "This is how we have always done it," we might say. That feeling, that instinct to protect the familiar, is the resistance Convexity asks us to examine. It is the discomfort of having our flat mirror, the one that reflects our history and comfort, challenged by a new perspective. At first, the curved view feels strange, even exaggerated. But then, if we are patient, something clicks. The curve starts to make sense. The margin for a new idea creates space. You breathe more. You see the other person's perspective not as a threat, but as a reality to consider. You do not just react; you respond. That is the gift of Convexity. It does not just widen your view. It reshapes your pace.

In the spiritual life, pace matters. God rarely moves at the speed of our certainty. He tends to move at the speed of awareness, of awakening, of invitation. When we move too fast, guided only by the narrow mirror of our own assumptions, we miss the quiet revelation emerging just outside our attention.

Convexity trains us to pay attention before there is impact, to adjust before we assume, and to notice what has not yet forced itself into our frame. It changes how we live, how we listen, and how we lead.

The Communal Nature of Sight

Living with that new awareness, I began to ask: Where else have I insisted on a flat view? What relationships have I misjudged? What patterns have I ignored? What voice of God have I mistaken for silence, simply because I was looking in the wrong direction? The answer was not always dramatic, but it was always humbling. Convexity is not just about seeing more. It is about acknowledging what you were never going to see without help.

We live in a culture that prizes individual insight and self-assurance. But Convexity reminds us that seeing clearly is rarely a solo effort; it is something we learn in community. We need other people to serve as mirrors for us, reflecting the angles we inevitably miss.

Sometimes the most effective mirrors are not the ones we expect. More times than I would like to admit, I have found that children make for excellent curved mirrors. Their genuine wonder and curiosity can cut through our adult certainties and reframe a situation with profound simplicity. They ask the "why" questions we have stopped asking. Their perspective has not yet been flattened by cynicism or routine. They are a reminder that God has a history of showing up in corners that rigid minds refuse to look. Consider Moses at the burning bush, an encounter that happened not in a temple but in a wilderness flame. Or Balaam, who was rebuked not by a prophet, but by a donkey.

When Jesus walked the Emmaus road after His resurrection, the disciples could not recognize Him. This was not because He was hiding, but because they had a flat expectation of what a resurrected Savior was supposed to look like. Their frame had no space for a King who shows up quietly, walks patiently, and waits to be recognized in the breaking of bread. Their vision had to bend before their faith could break open. That is the work Convexity does; it bends your categories just enough to let truth walk in.

This process almost always starts with humility. Humility is the fertile ground where Convexity can take root. It is the deep awareness that says, "I may not be seeing this clearly." It is the decision to step back, to adjust, to invite correction not as defeat, but as discipleship. The Apostle Paul writes in 1 Corinthians 13:12, "Now we see through a glass, darkly...." He is acknowledging that our current way of seeing is limited, partial, and shaded. We are always operating from less than full visibility. To live with Convexity is to remember: I might not be wrong, but I might not be seeing it all.

This posture is not spiritual paranoia; it is spiritual proprioception, a felt sense that there are angles beyond your immediate reach, and God may be speaking through them. In an age that rewards hot takes and quick conclusions, Convexity slows us down, inviting us to reflect before reacting. It gives us language for a more generous kind of accountability. Sometimes we do not need to call each other out; we need to call each other into a wider view. This is why Convexity cannot be a private practice. It must be communal. You need friends with spiritual depth and reflective presence in your life, people who ask inconvenient questions and offer loving resistance. These are the people who remind you that clarity is not the same as control.

If Convexity begins with humility, it matures through habit. It is one thing to acknowledge your view is limited; it is another to adjust it regularly, even when there is no collision. It is a practice, subtle and often inconvenient. It might look like asking someone you trust, "Is there something I'm not seeing here?." It might mean listening longer before you speak, or reading something that challenges your assumptions. Over time, these small acts cultivate what Scripture calls wisdom: not information, but formation. It is a way of seeing that allows space for what is real, not just what is familiar. It allows you to hold truth without weaponizing it and to speak prophetically without becoming performative.

It changes more than just how you process the world. It changes your relationships, because it reminds you that other people are not your enemy. They are your mirror.

You do not need to abandon your convictions, but you do need to hold them with curiosity. That kind of space is holy. It is where the Spirit whispers, where growth becomes possible, and where love stops being theoretical and starts being transformational. As we move forward, do not just read this book with your mind. Read it with your mirror in mind. Ask: Where is my field of vision too narrow? You do not need to fix your whole life. You just need to be willing to adjust your angle.

That is Convexity. That is where clarity begins. But before we can fully apply this grace-shaped way of seeing, we must first be honest about why our vision became so narrow. Because many of our most dangerous blind spots are not just bad habits; they are filters we were trained into long before we ever realized we were seeing partially.

18

Endnotes

1. Simons, Daniel J., and Christopher F. Chabris. "Gorillas in Our Midst: Sustained Inattentional Blindness for Dynamic Events." *Perception*, vol. 28, no. 9, 1999, pp. 1059–1074.
   — Referenced in discussion of inattentional blindness and the basketball-gorilla experiment.

2. Baars, Bernard J., and Nicole M. Gage. *Fundamentals of Cognitive Neuroscience: A Beginner's Guide*. Academic Press, 2010.
   — Referenced in the explanation of the Reticular Activating System (RAS) and perceptual filtering.

3. 1 Corinthians 13:12.
   — Quoted in reference to Paul's observation that "we see through a glass, darkly," used to establish the theological foundation for Convexity.

Chapter 3

What We Don't See

We All Carry Filters. The Question Is: Who Put Them There?

Some blind spots are not caused by mirrors at all. They are formed in us long before we ever get behind the wheel of a car. Long before we have words for concepts like clarity or curvature, we inherit lenses. These are ways of seeing shaped by our culture, our family, our pain, our privilege, and our religion. These lenses become our defaults. They are the quiet, invisible architecture of our worldview, defining what we assume is normal, what counts as important, who matters, and how to properly measure success. They whisper to us about who to trust and what to fear. They tell us what is worthy of our attention and what is beneath our notice. These foundational filters are invisible to us, at least until they are challenged. By the time we are old enough to question them, they have already shaped the way we see nearly everything.

We do not just have blind spots. In many cases, we have been trained into them.

This is why some people can walk into a room and immediately see opportunity, while others in the same room see only threat. It is why one person can hear a piece of critical feedback and use it to grow, while another collapses into shame. It explains how two people can sit through the same sermon, the same university lesson, or the same difficult family conversation and walk away with two completely different, and often opposing, interpretations of what happened. It is not always a matter of stubbornness. Sometimes, it is simply selective vision, a product of the filters we were given.

The Invisibility of Our Own Lenses

Psychologists call this powerful phenomenon confirmation bias. It is our innate tendency to seek out, favor, and recall information that supports what we already believe, while simultaneously ignoring, dismissing, or forgetting information that challenges it.[1] Our brains are wired for efficiency. They are designed to make sense of a complex world as quickly as possible, and the quickest way to do that is to filter out complexity and dissonance. We do not just interpret facts neutrally. We interpret them through the powerful lenses of our emotions and our memories, especially our unresolved memories. When a new piece of information comes into our field of view, our mind immediately and subconsciously asks a series of questions: Does this match what I already know? Does this make me feel safe? Does this confirm what I have already concluded? If the answer is no, our tendency is to dismiss it, even if it is true.

This process is not theoretical; it has profound, real-world consequences. Consider the tragic story of Dr. Ignaz Semmelweis in the 1840s. He was a physician who discovered that the mortality rate from childbed fever, a condition that killed many new mothers, could be drastically reduced if doctors washed their hands before delivering babies. His data was clear and irrefutable. Yet, the established medical community rejected his findings for decades. Why? Their inherited filter, their confirmation bias, was that a gentleman's hands were, by definition, clean. The idea that they could be carrying "cadaverous particles" from autopsies to laboring mothers was so offensive to their self-perception that they dismissed Semmelweis's life-saving evidence. They could sit in a room full of data, surrounded by needless death, and never see the truth.

Their blindness was not a matter of capacity. It was a matter of conditioning.

This is the very problem Jesus confronted again and again during his ministry: people with perfect physical sight but no moral vision. "Though seeing, they do not see," He said, quoting the prophet Isaiah (Matt. 13:13). He was speaking to people who were unwilling to see anything that did not match the frame they had inherited from their traditions. This is not just a problem for ancient Israel. It is for us. We have all internalized frameworks and narratives about who we are and who we are not, what is good and what is off-limits, what can be challenged and what must be protected at all costs. These filters are often well-intentioned. They may have helped us survive. They gave us language for the world. They offered us a sense of safety and belonging. But over time, if left unexamined, they can become barriers to the very transformation we need. Convexity confronts this conditioning. Not violently or through shame, but gently, like a better mirror. It asks, *What if you are not seeing the whole picture?*

The Scripts We Live By

Sociologists sometimes refer to these inherited frameworks as cultural scripts, which are pre-loaded narratives that we act out, often without any conscious realization.[2] These scripts tell us what is respectable, what is dangerous, who should lead, how to grieve, what is considered "too emotional," what is "doing too much," and when it is wisest to stay silent. Think of a traditional family dynamic where there are unwritten rules about conflict. The script may be to avoid confrontation at all costs, to never raise one's voice, and to allow disagreements to fade without resolution. For generations, this script is simply "how things are done." The problem is not that we have scripts; the problem arises when we treat them as infallible truth.

In the Church, this becomes even more complex, because we often inherit not just cultural or emotional scripts, but doctrinal ones. These, too, can become blind spots. We might be taught who God is before we have a chance to truly encounter Him for ourselves. We learn which verses are most important and which can be glossed over. We absorb subtle cues about who belongs in leadership and who is better suited to work behind the scenes. Over time, we can come to believe that we are seeing with the eyes of faith, when in fact we may just be seeing through someone else's frame.

This is not always malicious, but it is always dangerous. Because when our vision is limited by unexamined scripts, we can begin to defend our blind spots in God's name. We preach partial truths. We disciple people into legalism or license. We protect our own comfort by calling it conviction.

Think about Saul of Tarsus. He was zealous, passionate, sincere, and completely blind. He believed he was defending holiness. He thought persecuting Christians was an act of obedience to God. It took a literal flash of light on the road to Damascus, an event that knocked him to the ground and blinded his natural vision, to finally open his spiritual eyes. His first question, "Who are you, Lord?" (Acts 9:5), is thick with irony. The man who thought he saw everything clearly had to be physically blinded to realize how little he truly knew.

Or consider the Apostle Peter. Even after the resurrection and Pentecost, Peter still struggled with inherited religious filters. It took a vision from God, repeated three times, to help him see that the Gospel was not bound by the clean and unclean categories he grew up with (Acts 10). And even then, he was prone to relapse. Paul had to confront him publicly years later for reverting to a posture of exclusion when he came under pressure from his old, familiar religious community (Galatians 2). These were men of God, leaders of the early church, authors of Scripture. And they still had blind spots. So what makes us think we do not?

The Courage to Re-See

This is why Convexity is not optional for a life of faith; it is essential. It is not about doubting God's Word. It is about being honest about the lens through which you read it. It says, "My faith is not fragile; I can handle a more complete view." That shift, while unsettling, is sacred. It creates space for empathy. It teaches you to listen without bracing for a fight. It helps you to name the cultural water you have been swimming in for so long you forgot it was there.

Learning to see differently does not mean everything you once knew was wrong. It simply means you are open to something more, something more nuanced, more whole, and more real. Convexity is the courage to re-see without needing to be proven right all the time. It is the difference between clinging to a belief and considering a new perspective, between defending your position and discerning the truth.

When Jesus healed the blind man in Mark 8, the miracle happened in stages. After the first touch, the man opened his eyes and said, "I see people, but they look like trees walking around." His sight was partial, blurry. It took a second touch from Jesus for his sight to become clear. Some might see this as a glitch in the miracle, but perhaps it is something else entirely. Perhaps it is a picture of how spiritual clarity often works: not as an instantaneous flash, but as a progressive and layered process. Even in God's healing, there is a grace for blurry beginnings.

That is what Convexity offers. It gives you permission to see in stages. It honors the process of unlearning without shame. It does not rush your sight. It gives you the space to grow from seeing people as walking trees to seeing them as they truly are. And in that space, you begin to recognize how many moments you have spent interpreting reality through yesterday's filter. And that recognition, that grief over what we have missed, is holy. It means your mirror is bending. It means you are starting to see not just facts, but people; not just behavior, but stories; not just what happened, but what it meant.

What we do not see often shapes us more than what we do. The only way to recover that vision is through humility. The humility to ask, "What have I never questioned because it was all I had ever known?." Convexity does not ask you to abandon your values. It asks you to widen the view through which those values are expressed.

With this awareness that our vision is framed by what we have been taught, we can now begin to identify these blind spots by name. We will start with one of the most subtle and corrosive of them all: the quiet expectation that we are owed something more, a sense of entitlement that shapes what we simply cannot see.

Endnotes

1. Nickerson, Raymond S. "Confirmation Bias: A Ubiquitous Phenomenon in Many Guises." *Review of General Psychology*, vol. 2, no. 2, 1998, pp. 175–220.

— Referenced in discussion of confirmation bias and the tendency to interpret new data through preexisting beliefs.

2. Swidler, Ann. "Culture in Action: Symbols and Strategies." *American Sociological Review*, vol. 51, no. 2, 1986, pp. 273–286.
    — Reference point for cultural scripts and internalized behavioral patterns.

3. The Holy Bible, Acts 9:1–9; Acts 10:9–16; Galatians 2:11–14.
    — Referenced in the discussion of Saul's transformation and Peter's inherited religious filters.

4. The Holy Bible, Mark 8:22–25.
    — Referenced in the healing of the blind man in stages, as a metaphor for progressive clarity.

Part II – Emotional Blind Spots

Chapter 4

Entitlement

What You Think You Deserve Will Shape What You Can't See

Entitlement does not always sound arrogant. Sometimes it sounds like disappointment. Sometimes it sounds like exhaustion. Sometimes, and this is where it becomes most dangerous, it sounds like prayer. We tend to think of entitlement as a loud and demanding posture, one defined by an inflated ego and unreasonable expectations. And yes, it can certainly look like that. But more often, true entitlement hides in the quiet places of our spiritual lives. It masks itself in language that seems honest, even holy.

We hear it in our own internal monologues: "I just thought I would be further along by now." Or, "After all I have done, this is how it ends?" And in our most private moments of prayer: "God, I have served You faithfully... why this?." These are not always signs of outright rebellion. Sometimes, they are simply the voice of a soul that is confused because the outcomes of life do not seem to match the effort we have put in. And just beneath that confusion is a belief we rarely admit, even to ourselves: *I deserve more than this.*

That is entitlement. It is not found in its loudest form, but in its most subtle and corrosive one. Because this kind of entitlement does not just distort our expectations of God and others. It fundamentally distorts our vision. It narrows our field of view until all we can see is what we feel we are missing. And when that happens, we stop seeing what we do have. We stop seeing the needs of other people. We stop seeing the grace that has carried us this far. We stop seeing the goodness that is still present, right in front of us. Entitlement creates a blind spot by anchoring our eyes to a moving target of what we feel we are owed.

The Resentment of the Faithful

No matter how much we receive, it never feels like quite enough. No matter how far we have come, it feels like we should be further. No matter how God has shown up for us in the past, we find ourselves scanning the horizon for the next thing we believe He "owes" us. And when we do not get it, the silence can begin to feel like a betrayal.

In psychology, there is a framework called locus of control, which refers to the degree to which people believe they have control over the outcomes in their lives.[1] Entitlement often sits at the worst intersection of this concept: it encourages us to claim an internal locus of control for our successes ("I achieved this through my hard work") while assigning an external locus for our struggles ("This is happening *to* me; God or others have let me down"). This mindset sounds like, "I was faithful, so I should be flourishing," or "I obeyed, so God should have honored that by now." When things do not go our way, we begin to question the goodness of the entire system.

The older brother in Jesus' parable of the prodigal son asked this same question. While his younger brother was squandering his inheritance in a distant land, the older brother was doing everything right. He stayed home. He worked the fields. He obeyed every command. But when the celebration for his brother's return began, when grace came home with a robe, a ring, and a feast, he stood outside the house, offended. He was offended not just by the party, but by the principle behind it.

"All these years I've been slaving for you," he said to his father, "and never disobeyed your orders. Yet you never gave me even a young goat so I could celebrate with my friends" (Luke 15:29). That is the voice of entitlement. It is not just disappointment, but resentment. It is not just honesty, but a demand for equity on our own terms. And in that moment of grievance, he could no longer see the father's love. He could not see his brother as family. He could not see the grace that had always been available to him. He could only see the goat that was not. That is what entitlement does. It shrinks our field of view until all we can see is what we believe we have been denied.

The Anticlimax of "Enough"

The truth is that entitlement and gratitude cannot coexist. One demands, while the other receives. One fixes its eyes on what is missing, while the other anchors itself in what remains. When entitlement wins, it does not just alter how we see God. It distorts how we see ourselves and our own lives. We start equating our value with what we have achieved or what we lack. This leads to a particular kind of exhaustion, a soul-fatigue that comes from constantly chasing a feeling of "enough" that keeps moving.

There is a psychological term that helps explain this dynamic: the hedonic treadmill.[2] It describes the way we humans quickly adapt to new circumstances, whether good or bad, and return to a baseline level of happiness. You get the raise, the relationship, or the recognition you have been dreaming of, but within days or weeks, the initial thrill fades. What was once a goal becomes the new normal, and once it is normal, it is no longer enough to bring sustained joy.

I have a friend who leads an incredibly successful and vibrant congregation. For decades, his earnest and sincere goal was to build a great church, to grow it, and to reach as many people as possible. By all external metrics, he succeeded beyond his wildest dreams. A few years ago, his church was recognized in the nation's premier publication on church growth as the fastest-growing church in the nation. It was the culmination of a life's work. But he told me something haunting about that moment. He said, "After I saw the article, it was a bit anticlimactic. This isn't what I thought it would be."

His story is a powerful testament to the hedonic treadmill. He had reached the pinnacle, the very goal that had driven him for years, only to discover that the destination itself did not hold the lasting satisfaction he had imagined. This is the subtle trap of an achievement-based life. We assume something is wrong with us, or with God, when the accomplishment does not deliver the feeling we thought we were entitled to. But what if the problem is not what is missing? What if it is the mirror we are using to measure worth?

Convexity interrupts that cycle. It bends the frame of our vision. It helps us stop measuring our lives by how fast we are moving, and start measuring them by how present we are. It helps us remember that deep joy is not found in the next milestone, but in the margin of the current moment; in recognizing that every breath is a gift, not a transaction. When we believe everything must be earned, we stop seeing everything that has already been given. Grace does not function like a payroll. It is not a biweekly payment for hours logged and duties completed. Grace arrives unannounced, unbalanced, and often, beautifully unfair. Which is precisely why it offends the entitled heart. And yet, it is the very thing that sets us free.

Convexity is what gives us space to notice that grace. It helps us see our brother not as competition, but as confirmation that what was lost can still be found. It helps us see the Father not as a distant manager of blessings, but as someone who was always willing to share everything, as he tells his resentful son: "Everything I have is yours." The invitation was always open; the older brother just did not notice. This is the critical move Convexity invites us to make: to shift our identity from an earner to an heir. We do not have to hustle for God's attention. We do not have to prove our value through spiritual performance. When we believe that, joy becomes possible again. Not the fleeting joy of a finally earned outcome, but the quiet, sustaining joy of undeserved belonging.

Let Convexity do its work. Widen the frame. Check the mirror. Look again. There is joy on the other side of this curve.

Once grace adjusts our mirror from what we think we have earned to what we have already been given, our bitterness can begin to fade. Yet, entitlement often leaves behind a stubborn residue: a creeping discontentment that whispers even the good we possess is no longer good enough.

Endnotes

1. Rotter, Julian B. "Generalized Expectancies for Internal versus External Control of Reinforcement." *Psychological Monographs: General and Applied*, vol. 80, no. 1, 1966.
    — Referenced in the explanation of *locus of control* and the tension between internal and external expectations in entitlement psychology.

2. Brickman, Philip, and Donald T. Campbell. "Hedonic Relativism and Planning the Good Society." In *Adaptation-Level Theory*, edited by M.H. Appley, Academic Press, 1971.

— Referenced in the discussion of the *hedonic treadmill,* which explains why new accomplishments often fail to produce lasting satisfaction.

3. The Holy Bible, Luke 15:11–32.
    — Referenced in the story of the prodigal son and the older brother's response, which forms the theological spine of the chapter.

Chapter 5

Discontentment
When the Good Isn't Good Enough Anymore

Discontentment rarely storms into our lives. It creeps in. It does not usually announce itself as an act of rebellion; it hides inside our daily routines. It is the quiet, nagging voice that can smile at an answered prayer and still ask, *Is this all?* We can be surrounded by clear evidence of God's favor and still feel like we are starving. We can have the job, the home, the title, or the peace we once begged God for, and yet still feel a subtle sense of being off. Not wrong, just... off. It is like our soul is restlessly scrolling past something we cannot quite name. The blessing has arrived, but our contentment never did.

This is how the blind spot of discontentment works. It shrinks our field of view until the only thing we can truly focus on is what is not there. It does not erase the good things in our lives; it just distracts us from them. And the distraction is dangerously convincing because it often shows up wrapped in the noble language of ambition, improvement, and motivation. We start using words like *calling, capacity,* and *optimization.* We talk about our desire for growth. But if we are truly honest with ourselves, we are not chasing growth. We are chasing a feeling of *enough.* And the marker for "enough" keeps moving. What used to satisfy us now feels insufficient. What once grounded us now feels like a weight.

The Mirror of Comparison

Psychologists call this phenomenon upward social comparison, which is the common tendency to measure ourselves against those we perceive as doing better.[1] In our modern age of curated images and quantified affirmation, comparison does not just steal our joy; it reprograms the mirror through which we see our own lives. We begin to evaluate our own story through someone else's metrics. Their salary. Their visibility. Their relationship. Their rhythm. Their applause.

Consider the common experience of a young professional scrolling through their social media feed. They see a former colleague announce a major promotion, a friend post photos from a breathtaking international trip, and a peer from university speaking on a panel at a prestigious conference. In the face of these highlight reels, their own steady, meaningful work can suddenly feel small. Their own life, which was perfectly fine and good just moments before, can feel as though it is somehow behind schedule. The discontentment that follows is not born from their reality, but from a comparison to a curated and incomplete picture of someone else's. We do not just want what they have. We want to feel how we *assume* they feel having it.

This is what makes discontentment so deceptive. It is not always envy or pride. It is often a quiet ache for meaning that got misdirected by the mirror of comparison. The mirror told us that the next thing would finally bring satisfaction. The next move, the next affirmation, the next round of results. And when it does not satisfy us the way it was supposed to, we do not question the mirror. We question ourselves. We assume we are broken, behind, or less spiritual. We rehearse our gratitude, but the words do not stick. Our prayers become whispers of disappointment dressed in the language of praise: *Thank you, Lord... but why not more?*

When Miracles Become Mundane

This is not blasphemy. It is spiritual disorientation. Scripture is filled with people who struggled to see the goodness that was right in front of them. The Israelites in the wilderness are perhaps the clearest case. They were freed from slavery, protected by plagues, delivered through parted seas, and guided by pillars of fire and cloud, yet in the wilderness, they grumbled. They complained, saying "we had meat in Egypt!" as if their bondage had been a banquet (Exod. 16:3). Their vision had narrowed. Their memory had rewritten their past.

Their present provision, a daily miracle of manna from heaven, began to feel bland compared to the illusions of what used to be. What they could not see, because discontentment had skewed their sight, was that they were being sustained by a constant miracle. They were waking up in the middle of grace and still asking God, "What else have you got?."

This is a modern problem, too. Consider a couple who worked and saved for years to buy their first home. They prayed for it, sacrificed for it, and celebrated the day they finally held the keys. But a year later, the initial joy has faded. The blessing has become the baseline. This is the "hedonic treadmill" we discussed, where our brains adapt to new circumstances.[2] But then, social comparison pours fuel on the fire. They see a friend's kitchen renovation on social media, and suddenly their own perfectly good kitchen seems dated. They were content with their miracle, until the mirror of comparison told them it was not enough.

When that forgetfulness takes root, something more insidious begins to grow: resentment. We begin to resent the season we once celebrated. We begin to resent the God we once trusted, because He did not deliver the version of the life we designed for ourselves. This kind of soul fatigue is real and dangerous. It shows up as an exhaustion that no nap can fix, because what we are really tired of is the feeling that what we have is never enough.

The Secret of a Centered Soul

Convexity steps into that disorientation not to rebuke it, but to reshape it. It widens our frame when our world is closing in around what feels missing. It bends the mirror just enough to help us notice what is still here, the grace that is still working, the miracle we now call Monday. Discontentment does not always need a new deliverance. Sometimes it just needs a new perspective.

The Apostle Paul knew this kind of mirror. Writing from a prison cell, he says something astonishing in his letter to the Philippians: "I have learned the secret of being content... whether in plenty or in want" (Phil. 4:12). That is not resignation. That is revelation. Paul was not lowering his standards for life; he was reframing his sight. He had discovered a joy that did not depend on what was happening around him, because it was rooted in the God who was within him.

That is what Convexity can do. It does not guarantee our outcomes, but it grants us access to a different way of seeing: access to clarity, to calm, to contentment. This is not because our lives are finally perfect, but because our mirror has finally curved enough for us to see the good we were missing. The good that is here. The joy that is quiet. The provision that is unfamiliar. The grace that is subtle but is still holding us up.

Convexity does not stop our ache for more. It just frees us from the lie that "more" will finally fix it. Because it will not.

Only a better mirror will. Sometimes, contentment is simply the quiet strength to stay in the moment God has given you, to love your family without waiting for them to change, to live today without demanding it prove its value to you. It teaches you to stop filtering your life through what is missing, and to start honoring what is already enough.

So if your soul feels tired, not from a lack of work but from a lack of wonder, Convexity is your way back. You do not need a new life; you need new lenses. You do not need another answer; you need a better mirror. The kind that tells you, "This is enough. You are enough. Right here. Right now."

When we learn to see the grace that is already present, our restless discontentment can finally settle into gratitude. Yet, as one emotional blind spot fades, another often takes its place, one that feels less like a problem and more like a solution. It is the subtle shift that occurs when our renewed sense of purpose hardens into a certainty that no longer asks questions: a false confidence that feels like mastery but is just as blinding.

Endnotes

1. Festinger, Leon. "A Theory of Social Comparison Processes." *Human Relations*, vol. 7, no. 2, 1954, pp. 117–140.
    — Referenced in the discussion of upward social comparison and its influence on perceived lack and self-worth.

2. Brickman, Philip, and Donald T. Campbell. "Hedonic Relativism and Planning the Good Society." In *Adaptation-Level Theory*, edited by M.H. Appley, Academic Press, 1971.
    — Referenced in the explanation of the hedonic treadmill and the emotional futility of constantly shifting desires.

3.   The Holy Bible, Exodus 16:3; Philippians 4:11–13.
       — Referenced in the discussion of the Israelites'
      complaints about manna and Paul's contentment in all
      circumstances.

Chapter 6

False Confidence
When Certainty Outpaces Self-Awareness

False confidence does not look like a blind spot. It looks like momentum. It looks like clarity. It looks like conviction. It shows up in confident handshakes and crisp decisions, in firm declarations and unmoving opinions. We see it in the person who always has a plan, a verse, or a word for the moment. They are the one who can walk into a room full of ambiguity and somehow already know exactly what should be done. We usually do not question this kind of person. We applaud them. We promote them. We even seek to imitate them. But sometimes, what looks like strength is just certainty that has not yet been tested. And when certainty goes untested long enough, it can harden into false confidence, which is the unshakeable belief that you see more clearly than you actually do.

This is the state where our instincts feel unerring, our conclusions seem above question, our failures are dismissed as anomalies, and our assumptions are treated as gospel. False confidence is one of the most difficult blind spots to detect because, unlike insecurity or anxiety, it does not feel like a problem. It feels like mastery. It convinces us that others need our clarity more than we need their insight. It quietly tells us that our growth is largely complete, our blind spots are minimal, and our self-awareness is sharp. And that is precisely what makes it so dangerous. Because the moment we believe we no longer need correction, we have become unteachable. And the moment we become unteachable, we stop growing.

When we stop growing, our vision stagnates, even if our platform or influence expands. This is not just a leadership issue. It is a soul issue. We can be right often and still see poorly. We can succeed in our outcomes and yet fail in our awareness. We can lead others to truth and still be living in a state of partial vision ourselves. This is the paradox of spiritual authority: we can carry profound insight for others while refusing to receive it for ourselves.

The Novice and the Expert

Psychologists David Dunning and Justin Kruger captured this dynamic in what is now famously called the Dunning-Kruger Effect. It is a cognitive bias in which people with low ability in a particular domain tend to overestimate their competence.[2] In other words, the less someone knows about a complex subject, the more likely they are to believe they know everything about it.

We see this in a simple, relatable way with home-improvement projects. A person watches a few online videos about tiling a backsplash and becomes supremely confident they can complete the job in a single afternoon. Their confidence is high precisely because they are unaware of the vast complexities they do not know, like mixing mortar to the right consistency, accounting for wall imperfections, or properly sealing grout. In contrast, a professional tile-setter with twenty years of experience is far more cautious. They know all the potential problems that can arise and will approach the job with a humble respect for the process. The expert's confidence is disciplined, while the novice's is inflated.

The wise doubt themselves more often, not because they are insecure, but because they are in touch with the vastness of reality. They know that confidence without accountability is just presumption in disguise. This is where Convexity becomes so important. It bends our mirror away from self-admiration and back toward honest examination. False confidence is a mirror that only reflects affirmation. It shows us what we want to see: success, progress, influence, and control. But it conveniently hides the edges, blurs our missteps, and edits our motivations. Over time, we can begin to build a life, a ministry, or an organization around a version of ourselves that is not entirely true.

Convexity does not demolish confidence. It disciplines it. It does not shame clarity. It tests it. It does not silence our voice, but it softens it just enough to leave room for another. It asks us, *When was the last time you questioned your own certainty, not because you were wrong, but because you wanted to be honest?* That is not weakness. That is wisdom.

The Certainty That Sinks Ships

False confidence is not just personal; it is relational and systemic. It causes us to misread pushback as resistance, questions as threats, and silence as agreement. We stop hearing what people are actually saying; we only hear what confirms that we are still right. Once that feedback loop begins, the very insights that could have saved us start to feel like interruptions. This is how a ministry, an organization, or a family can end up being shaped by one person's unchecked certainty.

Consider a gifted founder who launches a nonprofit. The early years are marked by incredible success, and their vision and confidence are the primary reasons for that growth. But as the organization scales, that same confidence begins to calcify. The leader starts to equate their gut instincts with infallible vision.

45

They dismiss data from their team that contradicts their plans, labeling it a lack of faith. They stop truly listening, and a culture of silence grows. The very certainty that once built the organization now isolates its leader, creating a massive blind spot that puts the entire mission at risk.

This dynamic is not new. On a grand scale, we see this in the history of the Titanic. It was a marvel of engineering, hailed as "unsinkable." This was a statement of supreme confidence in human achievement. This collective false confidence contributed to a tragic lack of preparedness, most notably a failure to equip the ship with enough lifeboats for all its passengers. It serves as a haunting metaphor for how our certainty can make us blind to obvious dangers.

We see this play out in Scripture, too. The Apostle Peter, bold and beloved, was convinced he would never fall away. He told Jesus at the Last Supper, "Even if all fall away, I will not." Jesus told him plainly, "Before the rooster crows, you will disown me three times." But Peter doubled down on his own sense of strength, insisting, "Even if I have to die with you, I will never disown you" (Mark 14:29-31).

His confidence was not empty bravado; it was sincere. But it was not accurate. He did not know the fault line that ran through his own courage. When fear cracked it open just hours later, he denied Christ three times, just as Jesus had predicted. The confidence that once made him brave now made him blind.

What is so powerful is how Jesus restores him later on the beach. He does not crush Peter's leadership; He curves his mirror. In John 21, the resurrected Jesus does not ask Peter for another vow of strength. He asks him three times, "Do you love me?" With every question, He re-centers Peter's confidence, moving it away from his own performance and back to his relationship with Christ. This is what Convexity does. It re-centers our confidence not on perfection, but on dependence. It reminds us that spiritual maturity is not about being right all the time. It is about being open to seeing rightly, especially when we have been wrong.

One of the greatest signs that false confidence is at work in us is that we begin to avoid spaces where we might be challenged. We stop inviting voices that do not already affirm us. This avoidance is not spiritual discernment; it is vision distortion. Convexity trains us to welcome healthy resistance not as rebellion, but as a tool for refinement. It gives us the courage to trade the question "What will they think of me?" for the much better one: "What might I be missing?."

Confidence is not the enemy. But confidence without curiosity will eventually cost us more than it gives. The people who follow us do not need us to be flawless. They need us to be formable. They need to see that God can shape us in real time, not just in hindsight. They need to see that clarity and caution can live in the same voice.

This willingness to adjust our mirror is the antidote to the emotional trap of false confidence. Yet, some of our most powerful blind spots are not driven by personal ego at all; they are rational, disguised as wisdom, and baked into the very rhythms of our lives. This is what happens when an individual's unexamined certainty becomes a group's sacred tradition: a stubborn defense of the status quo, where the phrase "we have always done it this way" becomes the most dangerous blind spot of all.

Endnotes

1. The Holy Bible, Mark 14:29–31; John 21:15–19.
    — Referenced in the narrative of Peter's overconfidence, denial, and subsequent restoration by Jesus.

2. Kruger, Justin, and David Dunning. "Unskilled and Unaware of It: How Difficulties in Recognizing One's Own Incompetence Lead to Inflated Self-Assessments." *Journal of Personality and Social Psychology*, vol. 77, no. 6, 1999, pp. 1121–1134.
    — Referenced in the explanation of the *Dunning-Kruger Effect*, illustrating the cognitive bias that causes overestimation of competence.

Part III – Rational Blind Spots

Chapter 7

The Status Quo

The Bias That Keeps Us from Seeing Better Roads

Some of our most powerful blind spots are born not out of arrogance or emotion, but out of rhythm. They form in the quiet, unquestioned repetition of what has always been done. We follow these patterns not necessarily because they are good or true, but simply because they are familiar. The status quo is comfortable, predictable, and, at least on the surface, it feels safe. It is the inherited habit we never thought to question, the policy no one remembers writing, or the leadership style everyone endures because, as the saying goes, "that is just how we do things here." It is not an act of rebellion. It is a function of routine.

And that is precisely what makes it so dangerous. Most of us will not challenge what we have grown used to, even if what we have grown used to is broken, inefficient, or no longer serving its original purpose.

Psychologists call this powerful cognitive shortcut status quo bias. It is the preference we all have for things to remain the same.[1] Studies show that even when presented with clear evidence that a change would be beneficial, people will often stick with the current path simply because it is the one they know. It takes more mental and emotional effort to switch than it does to stay. And the longer a behavior, a system, or a belief remains in place, the more "natural" and "right" it feels, regardless of its actual impact.

When Success Becomes a Blinder

We have all seen this. We have all lived this. We have watched organizations defend outdated practices because "it is what got us here." We have stayed in personal patterns we knew were unproductive simply because, at the very least, they were predictable. The corporate world is filled with cautionary tales of giants who fell for this very reason.

Consider Blockbuster Video. For decades, it was an American staple, the undisputed king of home entertainment. In the early 2000s, a small startup called Netflix offered to sell itself to Blockbuster for a mere $50 million. The Blockbuster executives, comfortable in their brick-and-mortar dominance, laughed them out of the room. Their status quo, built on physical stores and late fees, was immensely profitable. They could not see the massive shift to streaming that was just around the corner. Their success had created a bias. They were so loyal to the model that had made them a giant that they were blinded to the innovation that would ultimately make them extinct. What we do not always realize is that the bias is not in our logic; it is in our lens.

The status quo functions like a flat mirror. It perfectly reflects what is directly in front of you, the reality you have grown accustomed to, but it resists showing you what could be beside you, around the corner, or even developing within you. It convinces you that all vision must be forward-facing, when sometimes the clearest insight comes from stepping outside the established lane entirely.

This is especially true in our faith lives. So many of us equate stability with obedience and familiarity with faithfulness. If a tradition has been practiced for generations, we dare not question it. But simple endurance is not the same as faithfulness. Survival is not the same as clarity.

Jesus spent much of His earthly ministry confronting the religious status quo, not with reckless rebellion, but with redemptive reframing. He healed on the Sabbath, He welcomed outsiders, and He told stories that disrupted deeply held cultural assumptions. The people who resisted Him most were not the morally corrupt, but the spiritually certain. They did not oppose Him because He was evil; they opposed Him because He disrupted a system they had built their lives around. He curved the mirror just enough to show them what their traditions had edited out. And they chose to preserve their flat reflection instead of embracing a fuller view. That same temptation lives in all of us.

The Unwritten Rules We Live By

One of the quiet dangers of the status quo is that it often disguises itself as wisdom. It earns our loyalty not through threats, but through the simple passage of time. A pattern becomes "the way things are" not because it is objectively working, but because we have grown used to how it feels. Once that familiarity settles in, questioning it can feel like an act of betrayal.

This happens in our families. Consider a family patriarch who for fifty years has been the quiet pillar of his family's strength. He was raised with an unwritten rule that he passed down to his own children: "We do not show emotions, because it is a sign of weakness." He enforced this status quo for decades, believing it was his duty to be the stoic provider. Now in his later years, he has had a front-row seat to the generational damage this script has caused. He has seen his adult children struggle to connect with their own families, repeating the same patterns of emotional distance. After witnessing a holiday gathering marked by silent, unresolved tension, he finally sees the bankruptcy of the old way.

At the next family dinner, he does something that no one expects. He uses his patriarchal authority not to enforce the status quo, but to dismantle it. He looks at his children and grandchildren and says, "I spent my whole life thinking that strength meant keeping quiet about what I was feeling. I see now that it has cost our family a closeness we should have had. I was wrong. The silence is the weakness, not the feeling." In that moment, the mirror curves for everyone in the room. The patriarch himself becomes the agent of change, giving the entire family a new kind of permission to heal.

We see this in our churches and institutions as well, when structure gets mistaken for sanctity and programs persist long after they have stopped bearing fruit. Jesus addressed this exact tension when He said, "No one pours new wine into old wineskins" (Luke 5:37). The problem was not the new wine; it was the old, inflexible vessel. The frame could not stretch to hold what was being poured.

This dynamic is not confined to antiquity. The history of science and thought is filled with examples of new wine threatening old wineskins. When Galileo Galilei presented evidence that the earth revolved around the sun, he was challenging a geocentric model that had been the status quo for over 1,500 years. The establishment resisted his discovery with ferocity, not just because it was new, but because it threatened their entire intellectual and theological framework. Their wineskins were too rigid to hold his new wine. Convexity teaches us to question the wineskin, not with cynicism, but with courage. It gives us the grace to ask, "This may have been faithful then, but is it still bearing fruit now?."

Abraham had to leave everything that was familiar to him to step into the new clarity God was offering. "Go to the land I will show you," God said (Gen. 12:1). He was not given a map to a land he had already seen, but a call to a land that was beyond the edge of his current frame. Status quo bias would have told him to stay, to be content with what had been handed down. But Convexity, the willingness to follow the shape of an unfamiliar promise, led him into the unknown, and through that, into his legacy.

That is the challenge we face, too. We will be asked to look again at our maps and ask if they are still serving the mission. Because if we do not ask those questions, we will keep repeating the same patterns and calling it purpose. We will mistake comfort for clarity. We will call ourselves consistent when we are just afraid to change.

When Jesus healed the man with the withered hand in the synagogue, He did it on the Sabbath. He knew it would provoke the leaders, but He also knew something they had forgotten in their rigid adherence to the rules: "The Sabbath was made for man, not man for the Sabbath" (Mark 2:27). The system was meant to serve life, not to suppress it. But when systems go unquestioned long enough, they begin to demand loyalty at the expense of healing. Convexity breaks that cycle. It asks: Is this still making space for God, or am I just repeating a version of faithfulness that is easier than change?

You do not need to blow up your whole life. You just need to let the mirror curve.

This courage to question the familiar roads we travel is a massive step toward clarity. But a system's status quo is only half the problem; the other half is how we, as individuals, navigate it. Even after we have questioned the "why" behind our routines, we can still fall into a dangerous blindness in the "how," a spiritual autopilot where our faithfulness is measured not by awareness, but by the simple, hollow satisfaction of having checked the box.

Endnotes

1. Samuelson, William, and Richard Zeckhauser. "Status Quo Bias in Decision Making." *Journal of Risk and Uncertainty*, vol. 1, no. 1, 1988, pp. 7–59.
    — Referenced in the explanation of status quo bias as a cognitive tendency to favor existing conditions over change, even when change may be beneficial.

2. Swidler, Ann. "Culture in Action: Symbols and Strategies." *American Sociological Review*, vol. 51, no. 2, 1986, pp. 273–286.
    — Referenced in the discussion of cultural scripts and inherited behaviors that go unquestioned.

3. The Holy Bible, Luke 5:37–38; Genesis 12:1; Mark 2:27.
    — Referenced in connection to Jesus' new wine metaphor, Abraham's call to leave familiar ground, and the Sabbath reframed as life-giving rather than legalistic.

Chapter 8

I Checked the Box

When Completion Becomes the Enemy of Awareness

There is a special kind of blindness that comes from thinking the task is already done. You signed in for the service. You said the words of the prayer. You went to the meeting. You read the daily verse. You fulfilled the obligation. You checked the box. And in that quiet moment of completion, something subtle but dangerous happens. Your mind moves on, and you stop paying attention. The underlying assumption is that if we have *done* the thing, we have done the *work*. But action is not the same as awareness. Motion is not the same as maturity.

We can do the right thing for the wrong reasons. And we can even do the right thing with the right reasons and still miss the point entirely. Because when we check the box too quickly, we stop looking for what else God might be trying to show us in the process.

This is a uniquely spiritual blind spot because it does not show up as rebellion; it shows up in our routine. It is the quiet voice that whispers, "You are doing great. Keep doing exactly what you are doing." And because it sounds like an affirmation of our faithfulness, we stop asking the hard questions. We begin to confuse our familiarity with the habits of faith with actual faithfulness. We mistake repetition for reflection and performance for presence.

The Heart of the Matter

Jesus confronted this dynamic often, especially among the most religiously observant people of His day. He quoted the prophet Isaiah, saying, "These people honor me with their lips, but their hearts are far from me" (Matt. 15:8). They were doing all the right things externally. They were keeping the commandments, offering the sacrifices, and attending the synagogue services. But their obedience had become mechanical. Their worship had become performative. The checklist of religious duties was complete, but their hearts were absent from the work.

The scariest part? From the outside, no one else could tell. To the watching world, everything looked holy. The prayers were eloquent and the language was righteous. But Jesus saw through the performance. He was not impressed by the activity; He was looking for awareness, for nearness, for depth. He was looking for the kind of obedience that flows from a heart of presence, not from the pressure of religious obligation.

In recent years, a term has emerged in the corporate world to describe a similar phenomenon: "quiet quitting." It refers to employees who fulfill the basic requirements of their job description, but nothing more. They show up, complete their tasks, and log off. They have not quit, but they have withdrawn their passion, their creativity, and their emotional investment. Their bodies are at work, but their hearts are not. This is a perfect metaphor for checkbox faith. We can show up to church, read our Bibles, and even serve on a committee, fulfilling the basic duties of a believer. But we can do it all while being spiritually and emotionally disengaged, having quietly quit on the vibrant, attentive relationship that God invites us into.

Convexity offers the antidote to this spiritual autopilot. It curves the mirror, not to shame our routine, but to reveal where our rhythm has become disconnected from our reverence. Because the longer we move on autopilot, the more likely we are to drift, even if we are saying all the right things and showing up in all the right places.

When the First Love Fades

This is not a new problem. The history of the church is filled with movements and moments where leaders have had to call people back from a faith of empty ritual to one of heartfelt reality. The Protestant Reformation, for example, was sparked in part by a critique of "checkbox" religion. Reformers argued that certain practices had, for some, become transactional ways of earning grace, rather than expressions of a transformed and repentant heart. It was a call to move beyond mere completion to true communion.

Jesus Himself addresses this exact erosion of the heart in His message to the church in Ephesus. He commends them for their doctrinal purity, their hard work, and their perseverance. They were checking all the right boxes. But then He delivers a devastating critique: "You have forsaken the love you had at first" (Rev. 2:4). They were not unfaithful in the visible ways. They were just... disconnected. Their hearts had drifted, and they had not even noticed.

That is the core danger of the checkbox life. It gives us credit for movement without requiring our attention. This hollowing out can happen in the most sacred parts of our spiritual lives.

- **In our personal devotion.** What was once a hungry desire to meet with God in prayer and Scripture can

59

become another item on our daily to-do list. The goal shifts from encounter to completion. We read the chapter to say we read it. We say the prayer to say we prayed. The love that once drew us to the quiet place is replaced by the discipline that simply gets it done.

- **In our church family.** Our initial engagement might be fueled by a genuine love for the people and the mission. But over time, that can fade into simply fulfilling a role. We show up because it is Sunday. We serve on the committee because we are expected to. We have conversations in the lobby that remain on the surface. We are participating, but we have stopped being truly present with one another.

- **In our worship.** We can stand and sing songs of praise, with lyrics we have known for years, while our minds are a million miles away. We can lift our hands in a familiar gesture without any corresponding lift in our hearts. The act of worship, which was once an authentic overflow of our "first love," becomes a hollow echo, a performance we go through without true adoration.

When we have lived long enough with a checked-box faith, we do not stop believing; we just stop beholding. We stop expecting the Spirit to move because we already have a plan for the service. This kind of stagnation does not always feel like rebellion. Sometimes it just feels like a tired faith, one that is still functioning and responsible, but is quietly withering beneath the surface.

That is why Convexity is so necessary here. It reminds us that presence is not the same as participation. That doing the thing is not the same as being shaped by the thing. It does not ask us to throw away our disciplines, but to breathe life back into them. It curves the mirror until we remember that obedience is not about proving our worth; it is about creating space for an encounter. Because in the Kingdom of God, faithfulness is never just about completion. It is about communion. And communion does not happen through checklists. It happens through sight.

You do not have to abandon your rhythms. You just have to let them bend your soul again. You just have to stop long enough to feel what you have been moving through.

When we stop just checking the box and learn to be present in our spiritual disciplines, we move from hollow motion to holy meaning. But this intense focus on our personal habits can create its own subtle danger. We can become so adept at managing our own spiritual house, all by ourselves, that we forget we were never meant to live there alone. This is how the rational blindness of autopilot gives way to the relational blindness of isolation, the quiet pride that insists it needs no one and sees no one, because it has become an island.

Endnotes

1. The Holy Bible, Matthew 15:8 (cf. Isaiah 29:13).
   — Quoted in the discussion of outward religious behavior disconnected from internal devotion.

2. The Holy Bible, Revelation 2:4.
   — Referenced in Jesus' rebuke of the church in Ephesus for abandoning their first love, despite commendable doctrine and endurance.

3. The Holy Bible, Luke 5:16; Mark 1:35.
   — Implicitly referenced in the theme of Jesus

withdrawing for solitary prayer and presence, contrasting the busyness of unchecked activity.

Part IV – Relational Blind Spots

Chapter 9

Islands

The Myth of Self-Sufficiency and the Blindness It Breeds

There is a certain kind of pride that does not brag; it withdraws. It does not shout about what it has accomplished. Instead, it quietly insists it does not need anything, or anyone. This posture often shows up looking like strength, even wisdom. To the outside world, it can look like composure, discipline, and a rare form of maturity. But inside, it is simply isolation.

Perhaps no character in literature illustrates this more perfectly than Ebenezer Scrooge from Charles Dickens's *A Christmas Carol*. Scrooge is the ultimate island. His self-sufficiency is a fortress built of ledgers and coin, designed to protect him from the world. His famous retort, "Bah! Humbug!" is more than just a rejection of Christmas; it is a rejection of the entire web of human connection, charity, and fellowship that the holiday represents. He actively chooses his isolation, coldly dismissing his nephew Fred's invitation to dinner and callously turning away those who ask for his help. He is haunted by the ghost of his past, remembering his choice to let his fiancée, Belle, walk away because he had come to love the safety of money more than the risk of loving another person. Scrooge is the very picture of a man who believes he is strong and safe, blind to the fact that his chosen solitude has become a cold and lonely prison.

Many of us have been taught, like Scrooge, that strength looks like standing on our own two feet. We have internalized the myth that maturity means not needing help, that independence is freedom, and that privacy is a non-negotiable virtue. So we build lives that minimize need, emotional exposure, and spiritual dependency. We even spiritualize our detachment, calling it "boundaries" or "discernment" or simply "being low-maintenance." But what we are really doing is hiding in plain sight. We do not want to admit that self-sufficiency is often just loneliness with better branding. It is not that we do not need people; it is that we have convinced ourselves that we are safer without them. Once that belief takes root, we stop looking for connection altogether. We become our own reference point, our own counsel, and our own comfort. And that is where the blind spot forms.

The Distortion of Distance

The danger of isolation is not just disconnection. It is distortion. The longer we live alone in our own head, with our own habits and our own rationale, the more our mirror flattens. Our blind spots expand because there is no one there to question our perspective. Inside the fortress of solitude, our own thoughts become our only advisors. Our biases go unchallenged, our fears are magnified without the calming presence of another, and our grievances fester without the clarifying light of a different perspective. We become the sole, unreliable narrator of our own story. Without other characters to offer friction or grace, that story can become dangerously distorted. Eventually, we can begin to think we see everything, when in reality, we are just not close enough to anyone who would show us otherwise.

This is why Convexity matters so much in our relational blind spots. It reminds us that we were never meant to see clearly on our own. Perspective is communal. Truth often arrives through the voice and presence of other people. Our blind spots will not shrink until we let someone else share the road with us.

To counter the myth of the self-sufficient hero, we can look to the real history of the Lewis and Clark expedition. Their celebrated journey across the American continent was a success not because of a single, rugged individual, but because of a deep and trusting partnership. They relied on each other's complementary skills and on the diverse expertise of their entire Corps of Discovery, including the indispensable guidance of Sacagawea. Their story is a powerful testament to a simple truth: great and difficult journeys are navigated through interdependence, not isolation. We were not called to become islands.

The Wounds That Build the Walls

For many of us, the default to distance is not a choice, but a form of protection. We did not start out thinking we did not need people. We learned it, one disappointment at a time. After enough betrayal, unmet expectations, or misread vulnerability, something in us quietly decides that it is easier to be strong than it is to be seen. This is not selfishness. It is survival.

Psychologists refer to this as an avoidant attachment style, a pattern often formed when our early emotional needs are not consistently met.[1] We adapt by becoming self-contained, minimizing our needs, and convincing ourselves that closeness is a liability. Consider a talented entrepreneur who, early in their career, was deeply betrayed by a business partner. The wound creates a subconscious script: "Relying on others leads to pain." In all future ventures, they keep colleagues at a distance and handle every critical task themselves. The script of self-sufficiency becomes a source of pride, even as it leads to burnout. The entrepreneur might tell themselves they are simply more competent or have higher standards than anyone else. They mistake their trauma response for a superior work ethic. This is the tragic irony of the island: the very walls we build to protect us from past pain also prevent future healing and connection from ever reaching us.

While this avoidance might preserve our image, it slowly erodes our soul. We cannot receive what we will not acknowledge we need. We cannot be truly known if we are never truly accessible. We cannot heal if no one gets close enough to see the wound.

But Jesus did not live this way. He did not build His life on isolation or retreat as a default. He surrounded Himself with flawed, difficult, and draining people. And at His most vulnerable moment, in the Garden of Gethsemane, He said to His closest friends, "My soul is overwhelmed with sorrow... Stay here and keep watch with me" (Matt. 26:38). This is a moment of profound theological importance. The one person in history who was truly self-sufficient, who held all power and authority, chose interdependence in His moment of greatest human anguish. His request is not a sign of weakness; it is a divine model of vulnerability. It sanctifies our own need for community and rebukes the false gospel of rugged individualism that many of us have been taught to worship. The Son of God asked to not be alone. If that is not divine permission for us to be human and to need one another, what is?

Convexity invites us back into that kind of permission. It curves the mirror enough to help us see that solitude is not always spiritual and that strength without connection is just a performance in disguise. The goal is not independence, but interdependence. This is not codependency or performative closeness, but mutual awareness, mutual covering, and mutual responsibility.

68

The writer of Hebrews puts it plainly: "Let us not give up meeting together, as some are in the habit of doing... but let us encourage one another" (Heb. 10:25). This is not about church attendance. It is about belonging. And belonging is not a luxury; it is a lifeline. The longer we stay isolated, the easier it is to believe we are clear-headed, when we are actually just uninterrupted. That is not clarity. It is blindness preserved by distance.

Reconnection does not happen all at once, but it has to start somewhere. Sometimes the most courageous thing we can do is let someone see us before we have figured everything out. Every step we take off the island reclaims a part of our soul that silence tried to hold hostage. You do not need everyone to see you. But you do need someone.

Taking that first step off the island and choosing connection is a courageous act of faith. But proximity introduces its own immediate challenge: once people are close enough to be seen, we must contend with how we see them. The very wounds that drove us into isolation can become the distorted lens through which we now view every action, causing us to assign motives that have more to do with our own past than their present heart.

Endnotes

1. Bowlby, John. *Attachment and Loss: Vol. 1. Attachment.* Basic Books, 1969.
    — Referenced in the explanation of avoidant attachment patterns, particularly how early relational disruptions can shape adult tendencies toward emotional self-sufficiency and isolation.

2. The Holy Bible, Matthew 26:36–38.
    — Referenced in Jesus' request for companionship and emotional presence during His time in Gethsemane.

3. The Holy Bible, Hebrews 10:24–25.
    — Referenced in the call to resist isolation and prioritize relational encouragement within the faith community.

Chapter 10

The Motive

When You Can't See the Heart Behind the Action

There are few things more damaging to our relationships than the quiet act of mistrusting someone's motive. We are not talking about their actions, which are observable, or their outcomes, which are measurable. We are talking about their intention, the invisible why behind what they do. Because once we begin to question the *why*, we stop seeing the *what* clearly. Every action, every word, every silence is suddenly filtered through a lens of suspicion. A short reply becomes clear evidence of disrespect. A missed phone call is interpreted as a silent rejection. A slight shift in tone during a conversation is analyzed as proof of a hidden agenda.

The more often it happens, the more a story begins to write itself in our minds, a story that solidifies without facts, without confirmation, and, most tragically, without any curiosity. We begin filling in all the blank spaces with our worst assumptions. And what we do not realize is that the story we are telling is not actually coming from the other person. It is coming from us. It is a projection of our own wounds, our own memories, and our own well-worn defense systems. It flows from a deeply held belief, one that is sometimes even spiritualized for its own protection, that says, "People simply cannot be trusted."

A Tale of Two Judgments

Psychologists call this near-universal tendency the fundamental attribution error. It is our habit of attributing others' behavior to their essential character while attributing our own behavior to our immediate context.[1] We see this happen every day in the simplest of interactions. Imagine you send a thoughtful, detailed email to a colleague about a project you are both working on. An hour later, you receive a one-sentence reply that does not address any of your key points.

Our default reaction is often to make a judgment about our colleague's character. "They are so dismissive," we might think. "They clearly do not respect my work, and they are probably trying to undermine the project." We invent an entire narrative of negative intent. But if the roles were reversed, and we were the one sending the curt reply, our explanation would be entirely different. We would tell ourselves, "I am completely overwhelmed today. I have three deadlines, and I just wanted to acknowledge the email so they knew I saw it. I will get back to it properly when I have time." This perfectly illustrates the double standard. As you so powerfully phrased it, **we grant ourselves grace based on context but judge others based on perceived character.**

This blind spot does not form because we are malicious. It forms because we are wounded. Somewhere along the way, trusting someone cost us something significant. Perhaps we believed in someone and were betrayed. Perhaps we extended grace and it was trampled. Perhaps we remained open and vulnerable, and it made us feel foolish. So, we made a subconscious adjustment to our lens. We stopped expecting the best from people. We started anticipating the harm, scanning for the threat, preparing for the inevitable letdown. And the less we named this internal shift, the more normal it felt. Eventually, our self-protection became a projection onto others.

Convexity helps us see that shift. It curves our mirror, not just to reveal what others are doing, but to help us ask the much more important question: *Why am I seeing them this way?* It invites us to consider alternative narratives. What if the way they said that was not meant to harm you? What if the silence was about their uncertainty, not your rejection? Convexity does not ignore wisdom or erase the need for healthy boundaries. It simply restores the possibility of grace. It helps us see that a heart closed off by suspicion is a distorted lens. Until that lens is curved by grace, we will keep assigning motives that have more to do with our own history than the person standing in front of us.

The High Cost of Misread Motives

Mistrust rarely begins with malice. It often begins with a misinterpretation born from our own pain. While this blind spot can poison our personal relationships, history shows us that when it operates on a societal scale, it can be used to justify horrific injustice. The Jim Crow era in the United States, which followed the Reconstruction period, was built on a foundation of assigning sinister motives to an entire race of people.

Based on deep-seated racial bias, the dominant white culture projected a host of negative characteristics onto Black Americans. They were perceived not as individuals, but as a monolithic group whose motives were assumed to be lazy, criminal, and inferior. Every action was filtered through this distorted lens. A Black man not showing deference was seen as a sign of aggression. A demand for fair wages was seen as an attempt to usurp the social order. These misjudged motives were then codified into a brutal system of laws designed to enforce segregation and suppress rights. This tragic period of history serves as a devastating example of the fundamental attribution error on a mass scale, where the context of a people struggling for freedom after centuries of bondage was ignored, and their perceived character was used to justify oppression. It is a stark reminder that assigning motives without curiosity or grace is not just a relational misstep; it can be a tool of profound evil.

Scripture is also full of stories that reveal the damage this blind spot can cause. Take Joseph and his brothers. In Genesis 50, long after the brothers had sold Joseph into slavery, and long after Joseph had forgiven them, fed them, and given them land in Egypt, they still could not escape their own guilt. After their father Jacob died, they came to Joseph in fear, convinced that he had only been pretending to be gracious. "What if Joseph holds a grudge against us and pays us back for all the wrong we did to him?" they fretted. They projected onto him the very vengeful motive that they believed they deserved. They could not imagine true grace, because they could not imagine it for themselves. Their unresolved guilt made them blind to the love that had been proven faithful right in front of them.

Or look at David and his wife Michal in 2 Samuel 6. When the Ark of the Covenant finally returns to Jerusalem, David is overcome with joy and dances before the Lord with abandon. But when he returns home, Michal greets him not with shared joy, but with cynical contempt. "How the king of Israel has distinguished himself today," she says with sarcasm. She saw his passionate worship and her lens of suspicion interpreted it as ego. She mistook his spiritual freedom for a shameless spectacle. And that one assumption, that one misread motive, created a distance between them that Scripture says was never repaired. One heart was left unseen.

This happens in our modern friendships, marriages, and churches all the time. We do not ask; we assume. We do not clarify; we conclude. We do not see; we filter. That is the heart of this blind spot: filtering our perception through our fear instead of through our faith. Convexity bends that filter. It does not ask you to excuse patterns of genuine manipulation. But it does ask a critical question: *Have I let one wound turn into a lens through which I see everyone?* If we keep assigning motives without asking for meaning, we will eventually surround ourselves with silence, not because people do not care, but because they have learned that we only trust our own negative narratives. That is not wisdom. That is loneliness.

Convexity reminds us that discernment names the truth, but it does not presume to know a person's intent. Wisdom watches closely, but it does not fill in the silence with fear. You can protect your peace without preemptively labeling someone's heart. You can set a boundary without building a wall around your soul. That is what curved mirrors are for. They show you what is at the edge of your perception, what your flat certainty might cause you to miss. They give you just enough space to reframe the story before it becomes a sentence.

You do not have to assume the worst. You do not have to assign motives. You can pause. You can curve the mirror. You can look again. You can choose to see with grace before judgment.

Once we commit to seeing others through a lens of grace rather than suspicion, our relationships can begin to heal. Yet there is another, more subtle relational blind spot that often emerges, not in how we judge others, but in how we elevate ourselves in comparison. It is the quiet superiority that grows when we believe our lens is not just healed, but has now become the clearest one in the room, leaving us with the settled and dangerous conviction that we have got it all figured out.

Endnotes

1. Ross, Lee, and Richard E. Nisbett. "The Actor and the Observer: Divergent Perceptions of the Causes of Behavior." In *The Person and the Situation: Perspectives of Social Psychology*, McGraw-Hill, 1991.
   — Referenced in the explanation of the *fundamental attribution error*, which describes how we tend to attribute others' behavior to character rather than context.

2. The Holy Bible, Genesis 50:15–21.
   — Referenced in the story of Joseph's brothers projecting vengeance onto him, despite his demonstrated forgiveness.

3. The Holy Bible, 2 Samuel 6:16–23.
   — Referenced in the example of Michal misinterpreting David's joy as arrogance, leading to lasting relational estrangement.

4. The Holy Bible, Matthew 26:36–46.
   — Referenced earlier in Chapter 9, but echoed here in the motif of misunderstood intention and emotional vulnerability in relationships.

Chapter 11

I've Got It All Figured Out

When Superiority Becomes a Shield Against Seeing Clearly

There is a unique kind of blindness that hides behind brilliance. It is the kind that does not need to raise its voice or demand attention. It already knows what is best. It has the right vocabulary, the right theological framework, and the right interpretation of events. It does not come across as insecure; it comes across as settled. It is the person who no longer asks questions, because they believe they have already arrived at all the important answers. They are more concerned with being insightful than with being open. They have forgotten how to listen without simultaneously preparing a response.

We see this archetype in many settings. Let us call him "The Expert in the Room." He is the seasoned professional or the long-time ministry leader who has decades of experience. In meetings, he is not listening to understand a new perspective; he is listening to find the flaw in it. He often interrupts, finishes people's sentences, or quickly dismisses a new idea because it does not fit into a category he has already mastered. His expertise is real, but it has calcified. It has become a shield that prevents new information, genuine collaboration, or the humbling possibility of being wrong from ever getting through.

And the most dangerous part? He usually thinks he is helping. He believes his clarity is a gift and his insight is a safeguard for the group. And sometimes it is. But when that insight goes unchallenged long enough, it stops adapting, it stops listening, and it stops being accountable to anything but its own echo. This is the blind spot of superiority, and it is subtle.

It does not always look like arrogance. Sometimes it looks like confidence. Sometimes it looks like mastery. But it is built on the belief that your way of seeing is the clearest, and therefore, the most trustworthy. And when you believe that, you do not just stop learning. You stop looking.

When the Framework Blinds Us

This is why the Apostle Paul issued such a stark warning about a certain kind of knowledge. He was not critiquing the boastful or arrogant, but the insulated. "If anyone thinks they know something," he wrote, "they do not yet know as they ought to know" (1 Cor. 8:2). In other words, the moment we believe we have mastered understanding, we reveal how much we are still missing. That is the paradox of true wisdom: it lives in the tension between confidence and curiosity. It carries conviction with gentleness and speaks truth without superiority. But when curiosity dies, humility dies with it. And once humility is gone, our field of vision narrows, even if our vocabulary grows.

Scripture is filled with people who said all the right things, and still got it tragically wrong. Take Job's friends. When Job's world unraveled, they came to comfort him, but their empathy quickly gave way to explanation. They began interpreting his immense suffering, framing it with what they believed was theological precision. They were certain that Job must have done something to deserve his fate. Their framework was airtight, logical, and scripturally grounded: righteousness equals reward, and suffering equals sin. It was also dead wrong.

They were not malicious men. They were confident men. They had a system that explained how God worked, and that system left no room for mystery, for exception, or for unexplainable grace. This is a historical pattern. In the 19th century, the medical establishment was certain it had disease figured out. The dominant paradigm was the "miasma theory," which held that sickness was caused by "bad air." When scientists like Louis Pasteur presented clear evidence for germ theory, the community of experts fiercely resisted. The idea of invisible creatures causing disease did not fit their established framework. Their intellectual superiority created a blind spot that delayed life-saving practices for years, costing countless lives.

Like those doctors, Job's friends could not see the truth because they were too busy defending their own understanding. At the end of the story, God does not rebuke Job for his honest lament. He rebukes the friends for their confident assumptions (Job 42:7). Their certainty had made them blind. That is what superiority does. It puts us in the position of defending our worldview, even when that defense requires us to misread someone else's humanity.

Or consider Jesus' parable of the Pharisee and the tax collector. The Pharisee stood in the temple and prayed, "God, I thank you that I am not like other men..." (Luke 18:11). His prayer was a technically accurate list of his own accomplishments. He fasted. He tithed. He did all the right things. But his posture was poisoned by self-comparison. He did not need mercy; he was the mirror. The tax collector, by contrast, would not even look up. He simply prayed, "God, have mercy on me, a sinner." And Jesus said it was he, not the Pharisee, who went home justified. Why? Because humility widens the frame. Superiority shrinks it until we can only see ourselves.

The Return to Wonder

This blind spot is so hard to confess because it does not feel toxic; it feels responsible. We are the ones who do the reading, the research, and the prep work. We are the ones people look to for answers. And somewhere in all that rightness, we can forget that we are still being formed. Convexity does not take away our clarity; it deepens it. It helps us ask, "Have I become more committed to being right than to being real?." "Have I confused my certainty with God's?"

The older we get, the easier it is to trade our sense of wonder for a set of explanations. We have seen things, lived through storms, and earned our voice. And slowly, without ever deciding to, we can stop sitting at the feet of others. We stop leaning in. We stop letting new questions open us up. We stop being formed and start settling into the version of ourselves that is already familiar. We become someone who knows how to speak into other people's lives, but who no longer lets anyone speak into ours.

But Convexity breaks through that insulation. It reminds us that we were never meant to be the final mirror; we were meant to reflect something, and Someone, larger than ourselves. True maturity does not come from figuring it all out. It comes from knowing how much still lives beyond our current frame. It comes from remembering that God has a long history of using unexpected voices to reveal holy things. He has used a donkey to correct a prophet (Numbers 22:28), a stuttering man to liberate a nation (Exodus 4:10-12), a boy with a slingshot to defeat a giant (1 Samuel 17), and uneducated fishermen to turn the world upside down (Acts 4:13).

80

Convexity invites us to become that kind of person again, not someone who performs certainty, but someone who embodies wonder. It is the humility to pray, "God, show me where I have closed my ears. Show me who I have dismissed because I thought I already understood." That prayer is the beginning of re-formation. It is how our strength becomes soft again, how our knowledge becomes worship, and how our leadership becomes discipleship again.

This posture of humility is what dismantles our relational blind spots, allowing us to see ourselves and others with grace. Now, with a curved mirror in hand, we turn to the final and most foundational form of blindness: the spiritual kind. For what happens when the person who thought they knew it all is exposed to more truth than ever, yet finds themselves more unchanged than ever? This is the quiet danger of hearing without heeding, where the sheer volume of God's Word can become a shield against its power.

Endnotes

1. The Holy Bible, 1 Corinthians 8:2.
    — Quoted in reference to Paul's warning about overestimating one's knowledge and mistaking certainty for spiritual maturity.

2. The Holy Bible, Job 42:7.
    — Referenced in God's rebuke of Job's friends, whose confident theological interpretations were incorrect and harmful.

3. The Holy Bible, Luke 18:9–14.
    — Referenced in the parable of the Pharisee and the tax collector, illustrating the spiritual blindness of self-righteous superiority.

4. The Holy Bible, Numbers 22:28; Exodus 4:10–12; 1 Samuel 17; Acts 4:13.

— Referenced as biblical examples of unexpected voices used by God to reveal divine truth.

Part V – Spiritual Blind Spots

Chapter 12

Hearing Your Way Out
When Familiar Words Stop Forming a Faithful Life

We have never had more access to the Word of God. We have more sermons, more devotionals, more podcasts, playlists, commentaries, apps, and explanations than at any other time in human history. And yet, many of us find ourselves in a strange and frustrating paradox: we are drowning in insight while starving for transformation. We know the language of faith. We can repeat the phrases from last Sunday's sermon. We quote the Scriptures. But somehow, what we are hearing is not fundamentally reshaping how we are living.

That is the spiritual blind spot we rarely talk about: the danger of allowing hearing to become a substitute for becoming. It is a subtle drift. It does not deny the truth; it just stops submitting to it. We hear something that convicts us, and our first instinct is to think of someone else who needs to hear it, or even to post it online for others to see. We read a passage that challenges us, and we underline it or highlight it in an app, feeling a sense of accomplishment for having engaged with it, but we do not actually digest it. We have grown accustomed to treating the act of spiritual hearing as a sign of spiritual maturity. But Jesus did not say transformation comes from hearing alone. He said, "Whoever has ears, let them hear," a phrase that always implied not just auditory reception, but a response from the heart.

Consider a common modern routine. A person wakes up and, while making coffee, listens to a ten-minute daily sermon podcast. While getting ready for work, they scroll through social media feeds filled with inspirational quotes and images. A notification from a Bible app delivers the "Verse of the Day" directly to their lock screen. By 8:00 AM, they have been exposed to a high volume of quality spiritual content. Yet, by the time they sit down at their desk, it has all evaporated. The content was treated like any other form of media, consumed passively and quickly forgotten. It has become the background noise of a busy life, familiar and comforting, but ultimately, not formative.

The Closed Heart

In Matthew 13, Jesus quotes the prophet Isaiah to describe this very phenomenon: "Though seeing, they do not see; though hearing, they do not hear or understand." The people He was speaking to had direct access to the living Word of God. They were physically near the truth. But they were no longer being formed by it. Their ears were open, but their hearts were closed. This is the spiritual version of a blind spot: hearing enough truth to become resistant to its conviction. We can become so familiar with Scripture that we can predict the point before the preacher finishes the sentence, and yet be so disconnected from it that it no longer has the power to shape our soul.

This is especially dangerous for those of us who serve others spiritually. When you teach or lead regularly, you can begin to listen to content primarily through the lens of how you might deliver it to others. When you disciple others, you can hear with a filter of responsibility, thinking of how a certain truth might apply to them. We begin to tune our hearing for strategy more than for our own surrender. And slowly, our own soul starts to drift, even while our ministry continues to produce. We are not disconnected from the truth; we are just no longer personally receiving it. We have stopped being pastored by the

Word because we have learned how to process it for others too quickly. We have developed ears that listen for structure and sermon points, not for a spiritual interruption from God. And that is when the blind spot forms, not because we stopped believing, but because we stopped beholding.

The Mirror of the Word

The Apostle James warned us about this kind of spiritual numbness. He wrote, "Do not merely listen to the word, and so deceive yourselves. Do what it says" (James 1:22). The deception he describes is not about believing lies. It is the much subtler deception of believing that hearing the truth is the same as obeying it. That is the lie of spiritual proximity. We are close to the Word, close to conviction, close to the power of God. But we are still living from our old patterns, because closeness is not the same as contact.

James goes on to use a powerful metaphor. He says that the person who hears but does not act is like a person who looks at their face in a mirror and, after walking away, immediately forgets what they look like. Imagine getting ready for an important interview. You do a final check in the mirror and notice a large, distracting stain on your tie. You see it there, clearly. Then, you simply turn away, walk out the door, and head to the interview, doing nothing about the problem you just identified. How absurd would that be? To see a clear problem and then immediately act as if you did not. James's argument is that hearing God's Word without responding to it is just as illogical. The mirror of the Word shows us something true about ourselves, about our need for change, and we deceive ourselves when we simply walk away unchanged.

When this happens, even our holy habits can become hazards. We go to church, but we do not expect to be pierced by the message. We read Scripture, but we are already looking ahead to the next chapter on our reading plan. We hear God's Word, and somehow, we leave untouched. We are hearing like someone who has already arrived.

Convexity comes in at this point, not to criticize our consistency, but to curve our posture back toward responsiveness. It asks us to listen not just for information, but for formation. Not just for insight that we can share, but for an interruption that we must heed. It makes us slow down. To pause when a verse stings. To stay with a passage that unnerves us. To ask, "What do I need to surrender here, not just understand?." Understanding without surrender is a half-blind faith.

Jesus concluded His most famous sermon with a parable about this very distinction. He spoke of a man who built his house on rock and another who built his on sand. Both men heard His words. The only difference was that one of them put those words into practice (Matt. 7:24-27). The storm that came did not reveal their level of knowledge; it revealed the quality of their foundations. Convexity helps us check our foundation, not just our comprehension. Jesus said His sheep hear His voice (John 10:27). But merely recognizing the voice is not the goal. Following it is.

There is a kind of healing that begins the moment we admit we have stopped listening well. Not because we are rebellious or uninterested, but because we have grown too familiar with the sound of holy things. Transformation is never passive. We cannot download maturity. We have to behold it. We have to listen until something shifts within us. We do not need a new passage or a louder sermon. We need a new posture, a softer soul. We do not need to hear more. We need to follow better. Let the mirror of the Word curve our hearts. Let our hearing lead to movement.

This call to move from hearing to heeding is the very heart of a living faith. But it begs a final, practical question: How do we cultivate a life of responsiveness, especially when seasons change and new blind spots emerge? We do it by embracing the truth that clarity is not a destination we arrive at once, but a discipline we must practice by continually and intentionally adjusting the mirror.

Endnotes

1. The Holy Bible, Matthew 13:13 (cf. Isaiah 6:9–10).
   — Referenced in the explanation of spiritual hearing without understanding, and the warning against desensitized perception.

2. The Holy Bible, James 1:22–25.
   — Referenced in the contrast between hearing and doing, and the metaphor of forgetting one's reflection in a mirror.

3. The Holy Bible, Matthew 7:24–27.
   — Referenced in the parable of the wise and foolish builders, illustrating the difference between hearing and practicing Jesus' words.

4. The Holy Bible, John 10:27.
   — Referenced in the line, "My sheep hear my voice," to distinguish between recognition and responsive following.

Chapter 13

Adjusting the Mirror
Clarity Isn't a Destination. It's a Discipline.

You have probably heard someone say, with a hopeful sigh, "I just want to get to a place where I can see things clearly." It is an honest and deeply human hope. But clarity is not a static place we finally arrive at, like a distant city at the end of a long road. It is a posture we must continually return to. It is not something we achieve once and then possess forever. It is something we must maintain, like a mirror that has to be wiped clean and adjusted again and again.

This is because life keeps shifting. Seasons change. New wounds surface. Success subtly reshapes us. Disappointments can quietly close us off. The relationships and challenges that stretch us today are not the same ones that will stretch us tomorrow. And if we are not careful, we will assume that the mirror that worked for us five years ago, the one that showed us our world so clearly back then, still shows us everything we need to see today. But it will not. Because clarity is not permanent. It drifts. It fogs. It narrows. Unless we keep adjusting.

The earliest versions of ourselves needed different mirrors than the ones we need today. The fierce independence that helped us survive a difficult childhood may now be the very thing that keeps us isolated as an adult. The certainty that fueled our passion in our twenties may have hardened into a rigid and unteachable spirit in our forties. Convexity helps us make peace with that evolution. It reminds us that spiritual maturity is not perfection. It is reorientation. It is the humility to keep asking: Am I still seeing this clearly? What angle have I grown too comfortable with? What patterns that I mistake for faithfulness may now be rooted in fear?

The High Cost of a Fixed View

These are not questions of insecurity. They are questions of stewardship. We must ask them because the stakes are incredibly high. An unadjusted mirror does not just lead to personal blind spots; it creates collateral damage. We have seen throughout this book how a single, unexamined blind spot can steer a life. When our mirrors remain flat and fixed, our entitlement can curdle into a resentment that poisons our gratitude. Our discontentment, fueled by comparison, can rob us of the joy in our God-given present. Our false confidence can lead to catastrophic failures in our leadership and alienate the very people who are trying to help us.

When our mirrors are fixed, we defend the status quo long after it has stopped serving life, becoming guardians of old wineskins that can no longer hold the new wine God is pouring out. We go through the motions of a checkbox faith, performing a hollowed-out version of devotion. We retreat to our self-sufficient islands, mistaking our loneliness for strength. We assign negative motives to others, projecting our own wounds onto their actions and creating fissures in our relationships. We settle into a quiet superiority, convinced we have it all figured out, and in doing so, we become unteachable. The cost is immense. It is the cost of lost connection, missed opportunities, and a faith that stagnates rather than deepens. This is why the discipline of adjusting the mirror is not a passive hobby. It is an urgent, necessary, and life-giving act.

The most spiritually grounded people we will ever meet do not have the fewest blind spots. They have the fewest excuses for keeping them. They have made a life of seeing again, and again, and again.

The Practical Disciplines of Adjustment

But how do we do this? How do we cultivate this habit? Adjusting the mirror is not a mystical event; it is a conscious and devotional practice built on practical disciplines.

- **The Discipline of Seeking Contrary Views.** We must intentionally step outside our echo chambers. This means reading a book by someone we are inclined to disagree with, listening to a perspective that challenges our own, or asking for the opinion of the person in the room we know sees the world differently. This is an act of intellectual humility that actively works against the hardening of our own certainty.

- **The Discipline of the Honest Question.** We cannot see our own blind spots, but others often can. This requires us to cultivate relationships with trusted, "curved-mirror" friends to whom we can ask a vulnerable question: "Is there anything you are seeing in my life right now that I might be missing?" This is not fishing for compliments. It is a courageous invitation for loving correction, and it is one of the fastest ways to adjust our view.

- **The Discipline of the Gracious "Post-Mortem."** After a failure, a conflict, or a difficult meeting, our instinct is to assign blame. This discipline calls us to a different practice. It is the practice of sitting down later and asking not, "Who was wrong?" but "What could I have seen more clearly?" This shifts the focus from judgment to self-awareness and turns every difficulty into a classroom for growth.

- **The Discipline of Intentional Silence.** In our noisy world, it is often hard to see clearly because we are constantly reacting. We need to carve out intentional space for silence and solitude, not just to pray or read, but simply to be still. It is in the quiet that the subtle whispers of the Spirit can rise above the clamor of our own anxieties and assumptions, gently revealing the state of our own hearts.

These are not dramatic, one-time fixes. They are quiet, everyday habits. They are how we practice Convexity. They are how we choose to remain teachable.

Becoming a Mirror for Others

As we learn to adjust our own mirrors, something remarkable begins to happen: our lives start to become curved mirrors for the people around us. This is perhaps the highest calling of a life shaped by Convexity. But it comes with a profound responsibility. To be a good mirror for someone else is not to be a critic or a judge. It is not about pointing out every flaw we see. It is about embodying a certain kind of grace.

Think back to the first chapter and the actions of my father. He did not approach me with an accusation ("You are not a careful driver"). He did not shame me ("How could you make such a simple mistake?"). He simply stood with me in a moment of shared presence, diagnosed the technical problem, and offered a better tool. He validated my effort ("I know you do [check your mirrors]") before he pointed out the limitation of my equipment. He was a perfect mirror because his presence was safe, his diagnosis was impersonal, and his motive was love.

That is the model for us. To become a mirror for others means we must first do the hard work of examining ourselves. It requires us to approach others with the same humility we hope to cultivate in our own lives, offering our perspective gently and without superiority. Our goal is not to prove that we are right, but to help someone else see more fully, to help them discover their own blind spot in a way that leads to life, not to shame. Our willingness to say, "I have had to adjust my own mirror, too," is what makes our clarity contagious. In our honesty, others begin to exhale.

A Final Invitation

The first time I installed that small convex mirror, it felt like such a minor thing. Just a curve of glass in the corner of a mirror I thought already worked. But that curve changed everything. It gave me more time, more perspective, and more peace. It saved me from accidents I did not know I was headed toward.

That is the power of Convexity. Not in its size, but in its shape. Not in its complexity, but in its consistency. It does not demand that you reinvent yourself every season. It simply asks that you remain teachable. To revisit what you thought was settled. To slow down just long enough to re-see what matters. Clarity is not a reward for the righteous; it is a rhythm for the responsive. It is not a status we attain; it is a muscle we must stretch.

So here, at the end of this book and at the beginning of your next chapter, let me offer you the question that will keep Convexity alive in your life:

Where is your mirror due for an adjustment?

It does not have to be a dramatic overhaul. Just an honest one. Just an intentional one. Just a shift curved enough to let the light of grace in again. It might be a relationship you have misread, a rhythm you have outgrown, or a belief that needs revisiting. Wherever it is, God is not asking you to be ashamed of it. He is just inviting you to adjust. To soften the certainty. To stretch your sight. To see others, to see yourself, and to see Him again with less distortion.

May you have the courage to keep adjusting. May you have the humility to keep looking. And may you have the grace to see again, and again, and again, remembering the promise that for those who are willing to see and hear, there is always more to be found (Matt. 13:16, Luke 8:18). Keep your mirror curved. Keep becoming someone who sees. That is where clarity lives. That is where humility protects. That is where transformation begins. And that is where the next road opens, not because you have mastered the mirror, but because you have chosen to keep it curved.

Endnotes

1. The Holy Bible, Matthew 13:16; Luke 8:18.
   — Referenced in the theme of seeing and hearing with attentiveness, and the repeated invitation to stay spiritually responsive.

2. The Holy Bible, John 10:27.
   — Referenced in the context of hearing and following Jesus' voice as an ongoing posture, not a one-time decision.

3. The Holy Bible, Matthew 7:24–27.
   — Revisited as a final metaphor for transformation through doing, not just hearing—the house built on rock as a life shaped by responsive wisdom.

Appendix: The Convexity Journal

A Guided Companion

This journal is where the ideas in this book become personal. It's a quiet space designed to help you move from reading to reflection, from insight to honest self-examination. There are no right answers here, only your answers. Don't rush through the questions; let them sit with you. The goal isn't performance, it's presence. Use this space to find your one blind spot and begin the sacred work of adjusting your mirror.

Chapter 1: The Spot

Describe a time you discovered a blind spot in your life. What caused you to finally see it?

_____

_____

_____

_____

_____

_____

_____

_____

_____

_____

_____

How do you typically respond when your perspective is challenged?

_____

_____

_____

_____

_____

_____

_____

_____

_____

Who in your life has functioned as a "mirror" for you? What did they help you see?

_____

_____

_____

_____

_____

_____

_____

_____

Chapter 2: Convexity

What does "widening your perspective" look like in this season of your life?

_____

_____

_____

_____

_____

_____

_____

_____

Where in your life are you being invited to adjust—without shame?

_____

_____

_____

_____

_____

_____

_____

_____

_____

_____

In what ways might you be resisting seeing something from another angle?

_____

_____

_____

_____

_____

_____

_____

_____

Chapter 3: What We Don't See

What's one belief, pattern, or assumption you've never questioned?

_____

_____

_____

_____

_____

_____

_____

_____

_____

What cultural, family, or faith-based filters shaped your
earliest sense of right and wrong?

_____

_____

_____

_____

_____

_____

_____

_____

Are there any voices you need to listen to more deeply—even
if they make you uncomfortable?

_____

_____

_____

_____

_____

_____

_____

_____

Chapter 4: Entitlement

Where in your life have you felt disappointed lately—and could that be rooted in something you felt entitled to?

_____

_____

_____

_____

_____

_____

_____

_____

_____

What's one area where you find yourself keeping spiritual score?

_____

_____

_____

_____

_____

_____

_____

_____

_____

What would it look like to reframe what you think you "deserve" as something to receive with grace?

_____

_____

_____

_____

_____

_____

_____

_____

_____

Chapter 5: Discontentment

What parts of your life feel less satisfying than they used to? Why do you think that is?

_____

_____

_____

_____

_____

_____

_____

_____

_____

Where are you most tempted to compare yourself right now?

_____

_____

_____

_____

_____

_____

_____

_____

_____

What are three good things already present in your life that you've recently overlooked?

_____

_____

_____

_____

_____

_____

_____

_____

Chapter 6: False Confidence

In what area of your life are you most confident right now?
Could that be a place where blind spots are hiding?

_____

_____

_____

_____

_____

_____

_____

When was the last time someone gave you honest feedback?
How did you respond?

_____

_____

_____

_____

_____

_____

_____

_____

_____

Where do you sense God inviting you to trade certainty for humility?

_____

_____

_____

_____

_____

_____

_____

_____

_____

Chapter 7: The Status Quo

What's one pattern or tradition in your life you've never questioned? Why not?

_____

_____

_____

_____

_____

_____

_____

_____

Is there something in your family, church, or leadership culture that might need to change—but no one wants to say it?

_____

_____

_____

_____

_____

_____

_____

_____

What would faithfulness look like if it meant disruption rather than comfort?

_____

_____

_____

_____

_____

_____

_____

Chapter 8: I Checked the Box

Which spiritual practices have become routine for you—and where might God be inviting you to re-engage?

_____

_____

_____

_____

_____

_____

_____

_____

What's something you've done faithfully, but not fully?

_____

_____

_____

_____

_____

_____

_____

_____

_____

What's one way you can bring attentiveness back into your devotional life this week?

_____

_____

_____

_____

_____

_____

_____

Chapter 9: Islands

Where do you tend to withdraw when you're hurting?

_____

_____

_____

_____

_____

_____

_____

_____

_____

_____

One Blind Spot

Who has earned the right to see the parts of you that feel most protected?

_____

_____

_____

_____

_____

_____

_____

_____

_____

What would it mean for you to risk showing up again—not with answers, but with honesty?

_____

_____

_____

_____

_____

_____

_____

Chapter 10: The Motive

Who have you misread recently—and what assumption did you make about their intent?

_____

_____

_____

_____

_____

_____

_____

_____

What past wound could be shaping your current perceptions?

_____

_____

_____

_____

_____

_____

_____

_____

_____

What would it look like to replace suspicion with curiosity in one key relationship?

_____

_____

_____

_____

_____

_____

_____

_____

Chapter 11: I've Got It All Figured Out

Where are you most resistant to being challenged right now?

_____

_____

_____

_____

_____

_____

_____

_____

_____

_____

_____

What truths have you taught to others that you may need to revisit yourself?

_____

_____

_____

_____

_____

_____

_____

_____

When was the last time you let someone else lead you into something uncomfortable, but right?

_____

_____

_____

_____

_____

_____

_____

_____

Chapter 12: Hearing Your Way Out

When was the last time God's Word truly disrupted your routine or reshaped your response?

_____

_____

_____

_____

_____

_____

_____

_____

_____

_____

Do you tend to hear for inspiration, or for transformation?

_____

_____

_____

_____

_____

_____

_____

_____

What truth have you heard often—but rarely lived?

_____

_____

_____

_____

_____

_____

_____

_____

Chapter 13: Adjusting the Mirror

What area of your life feels like it needs reorientation right now?

_____

_____

_____

_____

_____

_____

_____

_____

One Blind Spot

What rhythm, relationship, or assumption might need to be revisited?

_____

_____

_____

_____

_____

_____

_____

What's one mirror you feel God inviting you to adjust—gently, but decisively?

_____

_____

_____

_____

_____

_____

_____

Bibliography

Baars, Bernard J., and Nicole M. Gage. *Fundamentals of Cognitive Neuroscience: A Beginner's Guide*. Academic Press, 2010.

Bowlby, John. *Attachment and Loss: Vol. 1. Attachment*. Basic Books, 1969.

Brickman, Philip, and Donald T. Campbell. "Hedonic Relativism and Planning the Good Society." In *Adaptation-Level Theory*, edited by M.H. Appley, 287–302. New York: Academic Press, 1971.

Cone, James H. *God of the Oppressed*. Maryknoll, NY: Orbis Books, 1997.

Festinger, Leon. "A Theory of Social Comparison Processes." *Human Relations* 7, no. 2 (1954): 117–140.

Kruger, Justin, and David Dunning. "Unskilled and Unaware of It: How Difficulties in Recognizing One's Own Incompetence Lead to Inflated Self-Assessments." *Journal of Personality and Social Psychology* 77, no. 6 (1999): 1121–1134.

Nickerson, Raymond S. "Confirmation Bias: A Ubiquitous Phenomenon in Many Guises." *Review of General Psychology* 2, no. 2 (1998): 175–220.

Ross, Lee, and Richard E. Nisbett. "The Actor and the Observer: Divergent Perceptions of the Causes of Behavior." In *The Person and the Situation: Perspectives of Social Psychology*. New York: McGraw-Hill, 1991.

Samuelson, William, and Richard Zeckhauser. "Status Quo Bias in Decision Making." *Journal of Risk and Uncertainty* 1, no. 1 (1988): 7–59.

Simons, Daniel J., and Christopher F. Chabris. "Gorillas in Our Midst: Sustained Inattentional Blindness for Dynamic Events." *Perception* 28, no. 9 (1999): 1059–1074.

Swidler, Ann. "Culture in Action: Symbols and Strategies." *American Sociological Review* 51, no. 2 (1986): 273–286.

The Holy Bible. Various passages cited from the New International Version (NIV), English Standard Version (ESV), and New Revised Standard Version (NRSV), including Genesis 12; 50; Exodus 16; Numbers 22; 1 Samuel 17; 2 Samuel 6; Job 42; Psalm 139; Isaiah 6; Matthew 7, 13, 15, 26; Luke 5, 15, 18; John 10, 21; Acts 9, 10; Romans 12; 1 Corinthians 8, 13; Galatians 2; Philippians 4; Hebrews 10; James 1; Revelation 2.

About the Author

Eric J. Freeman, PhD, is an author, pastor, researcher, and thought leader whose work explores the intersection of spiritual formation, emotional intelligence, and public leadership. He is the founding convener of The Freeman Institute for Integrative Research, where he leads initiatives in homiletics, policy, and theological reflection.

A trusted voice in both sacred and civic spaces, Dr. Freeman holds a Ph.D. in Homiletics with a concentration in Social Ethics from Anderson University. His scholarship and pastoral leadership are deeply rooted in a vision of clarity that emerges not from certainty, but from humility, self-awareness, and communal accountability—a theme that animates much of his teaching and writing.

Dr. Freeman's published works include *Grimké's Gospel Echo: A Handbook for Preaching, Clear Faith: Eight Simple Truths Every Christian Should Know*, and *Letters of a Father to His Son Jeremiah: A Spiritual Journey to Meaning, Purpose, and Identity*. His latest work, *One Blind Spot*, reflects the heart of his mission: to help people see more clearly so they can live more freely—with grace, integrity, and conviction.

He lives in Columbia, South Carolina, where he serves as a senior faith leader and a guiding voice for spiritual renewal, community transformation, and courageous leadership in a divided world.

EricJFreeman.com

FⅢR

The
Freeman
Institute
for Integrative
Research

www.ingramcontent.com/pod-product-compliance
Lightning Source LLC
Chambersburg PA
CBHW030842090426
42737CB00009B/1069